ALBERTO ASCARI

ALBERTO ASCARI

FERRARI'S FIRST DOUBLE CHAMPION

KARL LUDVIGSEN

Foreword by Mario Andretti

Featuring the photography of Rodolfo Mailander

Haynes Publishing

To Aari with love

First published in October 2000

British Library cataloguing-in-publication data:
A catalogue record for this book is available from the British Library.

Published by Haynes Publishing,
Sparkford, Nr Yeovil, Somerset BA22 7JJ

Tel: 01963 442030 Fax: 01963 440001
Int. tel: +44 1963 442030 Fax: +44 1963 440001

E-mail: sales@haynes-manuals.co.uk
Web site: www.haynes.co.uk

ISBN 1 85960 680 6

Library of Congress catalog card number 00-134248

Haynes North America Inc.
861 Lawrence Drive, Newbury Park,
California 91320, USA

Jacket illustrations

Front cover: Following his five years with Ferrari, Alberto Ascari races for a year and a half for Lancia. His last race before his untimely death is the Grand Prix of Monaco in 1955, driving the innovative but demanding Lancia D50. (Jesse Alexander)

Back cover: At Monaco in May 1955 Alberto Ascari is only days away from the end of his life. A fine portrait captures a man at the peak of his considerable powers. (Günther Molter)

Frontispiece

At the Nürburgring in August 1953 Ascari looks into the camera lens with that blend of shyness and scepticism that is the essence of his character. Within his bourgeois exterior there is a powerful – even dangerous – drive to excel. (Rodolfo Mailander)

Contents

Introduction

The Man with Two Shadows. That was the title of Kevin Desmond's book about Alberto Ascari, published in 1981. Kevin's theme was that this great Italian racing driver cast not only his own shadow but also that of his father Antonio, who was killed in a racing car when Alberto was a child. There were striking parallels between their lives – and deaths.

When Alberto was born in 1918 his father's race-driving activity had yet to gather significant momentum. On 26 July 1925, the senior Ascari died after crashing heavily during the French Grand Prix at Montlhéry, seven weeks before his 37th birthday. He had lived for 13,463 days. When his son died at Monza on 26 May 1955 he had lived for 13,466 days – just three more than his father – and was seven weeks short of his 37th birthday. The 26th – twice 13 – had been fatal for both.

Superstition was part of the character of Alberto Ascari. He was wary of the 13th and the 17th. Double the 13th was also worth avoiding; bearing number 26 his Grand Prix Lancia plunged into the harbour at Monte Carlo only four days before his death. I describe his superstitions, including the importance he attached to his robin's-egg blue helmet. 'Passionate appeals were launched after a Monza Grand Prix,' wrote Erardo Mattuell, 'when his helmet ended up in a fan's hands. Ascari begged us immediately after the race to publish a notice in the newspaper. He telephoned us there and came just after midnight to see the first copies and when it was returned a few days later he was overjoyed.'

Ferrari racing director Romolo Tavoni remembered a similar incident during tests at the track in Modena: 'Alberto put his helmet on the pit wall with the opening down, as it is when worn. Mechanics were working hard, going here and there and moving tools and components. Luigi Bazzi took the helmet and not only moved it out of that active zone but put it some metres from there *upside down* on the wall! When Alberto saw it he didn't make a fuss, didn't raise his voice, just inverted his helmet and calmly told Bazzi that nobody should touch it, for it was the most important tool of his job. Then he invented some pretext and left, refusing to continue with the test session. He came back the next day.'

The ominous parallels with his father's life and death have not been created with hindsight. Alberto was aware of them during his lifetime. Said his friend Mila Schön, 'The loss of his father wounded him in the innermost depths of his soul. He never talked about it but he could not forget it.' Other friends, wrote Desmond, his wife 'Mietta, Gigi Villoresi, Gilberto Colombo and Aurelio Lampredi all confirmed that Alberto had a superstitious fear of entering his 37th year because this was the age in which his father, Antonio, had been killed at Montlhéry.'

Against this background Ascari's actions that fateful week of May 1955 were all the more baffling, as Tavoni said: 'Above all he considered his blue helmet as a talisman: he would never drive without it. So when I heard that for his last drive he had worn Castellotti's helmet, I wouldn't believe it. It seemed impossible. For those who knew Alberto this is still inexplicable.' He had not gone to Monza that day expecting to drive so had not brought his kit. Logically, in such circumstances he would have abjured driving.

At the time of Alberto's death no-one dared to suggest that the great master had made a mistake. It seemed impossible. Rather it was hypothesised that his tie had flown in his face, that a strong crosswind had hit, that he had swerved to miss a workman crossing the road, that he had suffered a blackout following his accident the weekend before, that a wheel rim had dug into the asphalt or that he was simply fated to die then and there. No wiser than others, I suspect Ascari found the completely unfamiliar Ferrari sports car less biddable than he expected at a critical turn on the Monza track. This is based both on the reports of those who have crashed in such Ferraris and lived to tell of it and on my own experience at the wheel of a similar car.

The poignancy of the Ascari story is portrayed in these pages by the many willing eyewitnesses who so loved this remarkable man that they were eager to provide their tiles of the mosaic that was his life. Kevin Desmond comes first in that long queue. When I contacted him he not only gave me carte blanche to draw on many interviews he had conducted for his book but also sent photos he had been unable to include in it.

Tied at first in the queue is Gianni Cancellieri. I first met Gianni when we worked together on Ferrari's 50th anniversary book. Needing to interview people who knew Ascari, I asked Gianni if he would help from his base in Milan. He did so, in spades. Much of the direct testimony in this volume is the result of the interviews conducted by Gianni, whose knowledge of this era of racing in Italy is unrivalled.

Other testimony was provided by contemporary reporting. This was available both in the Ludvigsen Library and in the archives of the Museo Carlo Biscaretti in Turin. There I am in debt to Donatella Biffignandi. At Ferrari and Maserati, where Riccardo Andreoni and Ermanno Cozza respectively assisted with photos and information.

I am grateful for the photos taken of Ascari by Rodolfo Mailander. They inspired the creation of this book. Other important illustrative contributions have been made by Jesse Alexander, Bernard Cahier, Günther Molter, Maurice Louche and others credited as appropriate. At the Library its director, Paul Parker, has rendered valuable help in picture research.

At Haynes I have had the valued help and guidance of Darryl Reach, Mark Hughes, Alison Roelich and Flora Myer, to name only those who have been most directly involved in the creation of this book. My colleagues at Ludvigsen Associates must be thanked for their tolerance of my preoccupation with a racing driver's career. Above all I express my thanks to my wife Annette for her encouragement and support.

Beginning in 1997 with a book about Stirling Moss, we have now developed a series featuring great drivers. That these men have much in common was attested to by Alberto Ascari: 'There exists among racing drivers throughout the world a strange sentimental affinity, a sense of solidarity that often people do not understand. This is that the racing driver has two different attitudes vis-à-vis his rivals. During a race he battles with animosity and fury, without pity, against his antagonist and he is ready to risk his life to obtain victory. In everyday life, though, he is chivalrous and sincerely affectionate. Off track we become friends again. They know they can count on me in every situation and for my part I am assured of their affection and their reliability.'

'I never met him, but he had a greater influence on my life than anyone else.' So spoke Mario Andretti about Ascari. Mario kindly allowed me to use a text originally written for his 1994 book, *Andretti*, as a Foreword to this volume. Again, the personality of Alberto Ascari has inspired this valuable co-operation.

Ascari is remembered well. Is there unfinished business in this respect? His wife thought so. Asked if she had any desires, she answered 'Yes, that the Monza racing track is named after Alberto Ascari. He was one of the greatest Italian drivers and moreover he was from Milan: I think that's sufficient grounds.' I agree.

Karl Ludvigsen, Islington, London, 2000

Foreword

by Mario Andretti

1978 World Champion Driver and four-times USAC/CART Champion

Alberto Ascari was cool. That's what I used to love about him. He was described as having ice-cold blood. When I saw photographs of him in action, I could see he had a certain flair. He was quick, yes, but he was cool. And he was doing it with control and a style that was all his own. It was really appealing to a young kid.

I first became interested in motor racing when I was probably 11 or 12. You have to understand, in those days motor racing was more popular than any other sport in Italy.

That was especially true in the 1950s, when you had Ferrari, Maserati, and Alfa Romeo. They were the standards for racing around the world. Also, the first World Champion was an Italian, Nino Farina. And the World Champion when I was growing up in the early 1950s was Alberto Ascari. He became my idol.

In Italy, all that my twin brother, Aldo, and I had was the radio and the newsreels we'd see at the movies. There was no television. In fact, I used to go to movies just to see the newsreels because that was the only time you could see racing in action.

We were sophisticated enough to know the schedule and I used to buy the racing magazines every week. So I was pretty much up on what was happening. In those days there were not as many races, but the coverage was there. And I was always looking forward to the next race.

But it all hadn't sunk in yet. I knew there was something going on out there. There were guys doing it and I knew I wanted to be one of them.

Just the looks of the cars, the drivers, and their gear, all of that fascinated me. For me, it all started with the goggles, the kind I wore when I first started racing. They were just like the ones Ascari wore.

He was the best, no question. He was winning, and that's really what attracted me to him. There were other guys I loved to watch race, but they were not my role models. They might have been doing well, but my role model was the guy doing the winning. For some people, winning is all they'll accept. It becomes ingrained in them. I see a lot of that in my son Michael. And it was that way with me.

You look at my record over the years, and I've had a lot of races where either I won or I was right there. But if I didn't win, it didn't mean a thing. Second and third didn't matter to me. Which is not always the best way to look at things. I don't always condone that kind of thinking. Sometimes you can be a little smarter, a little more patient, and still be satisfied. You develop that with maturity, an element that ultimately works in your favour.

But in the beginning, man, I had to win. I *had* to win. Sometimes that desire cost me by spinning or getting into crashes. At the same time, looking at the whole picture and what that aggression delivered for me, what it got me over the years, I think if I had approached racing any other way I probably wouldn't have succeeded.

In my case, I couldn't have it all. I couldn't be patient and, at the same time, maintain my aggression. I had to be one or the other. As I said, it's not the best quality. Sometimes I wish I would have come to that realisation sooner. But again, that was my style, and that's what I had to live with.

It's hard to assess whether there is much of Ascari in me. But I hope the best in me is what Ascari had in him.

CHAPTER 1

It ran in the family

The story is familiar enough. Young man is motor-crazy. Defies his mother to leap astride a borrowed motorbike and roar around a city square to satisfy his craving for speed. Neglects his studies, yet convinces his parents to let him compete in motorcycle racing. It's familiar enough – but in this case with a big exception. The young man answers to one of the greatest names in his nation's motorsporting tradition. Alberto Ascari's celebrated surname helps him take those first difficult yet crucial steps toward motor-racing success. After that, however, he is on his own.

The son of auto dealer and racer Antonio Ascari and the former Elisa Marelli, Alberto and his three-years-older sister Amedea lived at Corso Sempione 60 in Milan. They were above the shop, so to speak – Antonio's Alfa Romeo dealership, the general agency for Lombardy. The robust lad took after his mother with his dark hair and his calm, jovial look. He stood out in a crowd with his rolling gait. Some thought him 'a boy with the dignity of a man'.

The 18-year-old Alberto Ascari is astride his Sertum, centre, for one of his first official motorcycling contests. He eagerly awaits the starting signal.

Alberto began his schooling as a boarder at the Longone National College, not far from his home. Entertainment on his breaks from school consisted of visits to the many car and motorcycle workshops in and around his neighbourhood, for the lad was obsessed with power and speed. This was easy enough to understand, because this was the religion in which his father was, if not the Pope, at least a bishop. One of three brothers and a sister, Antonio Ascari had begun racing seriously in 1919 at the age of 32 and by 1920 was driving the Alfa Romeos with which he would be indelibly associated.

His commercial links with Alfa helped Antonio Ascari influence its product policy. In 1921 he inspired its launch of the 20/30 ES Sports, which not only sold well but served as a basis for racing cars that could hold the fort until the pukka P2 designed by ex-Fiat man Vittorio Jano was ready to compete – and win – in 1924. Jano's move from Turin to Alfa in Milan was engineered by Enzo Ferrari, for whom the decade-older Ascari was a role model. 'If he came upon a technical problem that he couldn't crack,' Ferrari said of Ascari, 'he was not afraid to ask for advice or suggestions from someone who knew more than he did.' It was a quality Ferrari might have sought to emulate more often, if only to engage the sympathy of his collaborators.

The breakthrough season for Antonio Ascari, called 'blond and bull-like' with the bold jaw of an Egyptian sphinx, was 1924. In June at Cremona he won a 200-mile race at a speed just over 100mph with the Alfa P2 and was clocked at 121mph over ten kilometres – impressive for a car of only 2 litres. He was not, a reporter wrote, one of the 'many over-inflated balls' among the drivers of the day. Ascari represented a 'school of his own' with a style that was 'calm, safe, vigorous and valorous'. Later that year he won the Italian GP at Monza, then in its third year, and in 1925 he was victorious at Spa in the European Grand Prix.

The calmness and safety of Ascari's style were sometimes in dispute. The Monza officials went so far as to warn Alfa that the driver would be unwelcome there unless he moderated his 'impetuous' style and stopped cornering 'dangerously'. 'You see,' explained the driver himself, 'the difficult thing is not letting yourself – how can I say? – be tempted … charmed by speed. It's like being in a big tube. But you have to resist.'

Journalist Sandro Ferretti said at the time that Ascari's 'apparent audacity was the fruit of the methodical training that he conducted, scrupulously and zealously, over the route of every race.' He knew the road so well, in other words, that he exploited it more fully than less assiduous drivers could.

Antonio Ascari brought both an 'exceptional physique and inextinguishable passion' to his race driving, Ferretti continued, adding, 'the smile on his lips, a bit sceptical, was a reflection of his profound generosity. When he spoke of his family, his broad face was illuminated by a serene and radiant glow.' He welcomed little Alberto to the pits and the races, where he posed in his sailor's suit with his successful father.

Alberto was only five in 1923 when, on park roads in Milan, his father plunked him on his thighs, presented him with the steering wheel of his RL Alfa and said, 'Now you drive'. Undaunted, already experienced with his own pedal car, the lad gripped and turned with confidence. 'He'll be an ace,' bragged his proud dad. Later at Monza after a day of testing the Alfa P2 young Alberto again perched in his father's lap to guide one of Italy's finest racing cars around its newest track. Small wonder he was captivated by speed!

Antonio Ascari was in search of a hat-trick third GP win in a row when, on a Friday, he left his family at their villa on Lago Maggiore to travel to Paris to compete in the 1925 French Grand Prix over the 7.7-mile Montlhéry track on the city's outskirts. The race started at 8:00am on Sunday 26 July. With the rest of the Alfa team Ascari had already tested at Montlhéry, honing his precise knowledge of the demanding circuit. This helped him leap into an immediate and commanding lead.

After a 15th-lap pit stop for fuel and rear tyres Ascari retained his lead. A light rain began falling. Starting his 23rd lap he gestured with his right hand in front of his pit, expressing confidence. He did not complete the lap. On a fast left-hand bend a knock-off hub clipped a post retaining wooden palisades and Antonio Ascari's P2 went out of control, flipping several times before coming to rest upside-down in a ditch at the side of the road, carrying the driver with it. Mercifully, riding mechanics were no longer mandatory. Grievously wounded, Ascari died before his ambulance had travelled a kilometre from the gates of the circuit. It was not yet afternoon. In his honour the Alfa team retired its other two cars, one of which was leading.

Only 13 days earlier the family had celebrated the seventh birthday of Alberto. Now it was the youngster's duty to attend his father's laying-out in Milan and the procession on 30 July to that city's Monumental Cemetery. 'He was following with a serious and sad expression the coffin of his great father Antonio,' recalled racer and editor Giovanni Lurani. 'Giulio Ramponi, Antonio's faithful mechanic, was holding his hand, and I, an adolescent at that time, was never to forget those fixed, sad eyes of the very young Alberto.'

Italy's automotive establishment called to pay their respects to Elisa and her children. Among them was Antonio's team-mate Giuseppe Campari. Alberto, wrote Griff Borgeson, 'never forgot how the burly giant picked him up, held him in his arms and said, "Some day you will arrive at the heights as he did. Perhaps you will be even more famous." He kissed the boy on both cheeks and brusquely left.'

Alberto's wife would later doubt that he was inspired to race by recollections of his father's career: 'I don't think so. My husband was left an orphan at seven, too small to leave a lasting memory. Moreover his mother reacted in the opposite way to me 30 years later: she sent her children away. Alberto lived in boarding schools until he was 18.' Yet as the son of Antonio Ascari he was bound to be sought out by the world of racing, even if he chose not to pursue it – which in fact he did. His father had succumbed to the temptation ... the charm of speed. Now he was under its spell.

Elisa Ascari bore a weighty responsibility. She and her family were well enough off, although she no longer shared in the earnings of the Alfa franchise, which was managed by an Ascari brother. She ruled with rigour the lives of her youngsters. 'His mother was so severe! And not only when Alberto was a kid,' recalled friend and motorcycle racer Umberto Masetti. 'I remember once at a restaurant he phoned his mother. When he came back to our table he snorted and said: "Oh, dear mummy, what a dressing-down!" "A dressing-down?" I asked. "Yes, you know she's a real *maresciallo*."' She may have had the manner of a field marshal, but Elisa also had a weakness as Alberto himself explained: 'In a certain sense she had got used to the atmosphere of racing. My father had trained her, one might say.' He was not slow to exploit this.

On one of his school breaks Alberto befriended a neighbourhood mechanic, Goliardo Bassetti, who let him take his first laps of a Milan plaza on a motorcycle. This fuelled a heady craving which Alberto needed to satisfy. At school, the youngster told his mother, some bad boys kept stealing his Greek dictionary – five times in a row. With their replacements he headed for used-book dealers. From the proceeds of their sale he funded rentals of motorcycles for periods long and short, the longer ones sufficing even for trips to Monza north of Milan. The inevitable scrapes and scratches of an enthusiastic motorcyclist were dressed and bandaged in the utmost secrecy by Alberto's confidential nurse, his sister, until she too was banished to boarding school.

At age 14 Alberto sought to negotiate with the *maresciallo*. He would apply himself to his studies if, when he passed the vital gymnasium exams, she would allow him to have a motorcycle. She cagily withheld her commitment, but he did well enough for her to agree to the purchase of a big machine, a twin-cylinder 500cc Sertum. 'Smaller displacements were of absolutely no interest to this lad,' wrote Nino Nutrizio, 'in whom his paternal bloodlines were evident.'

After he achieved this objective, Alberto lost interest in education. Elisa responded by packing him off to boarding school in Arezzo, keeping the big Sertum back in Milan. Alberto and Arezzo soon fell out so Elisa sent him even farther away to a tougher science school in Macerata, 260 miles away. From there he escaped again, dressed in mufti under his school uniform, which he discarded before boarding the train for Milan. This set the Macerata authorities on a vain search for a crazy naked schoolboy.

Now mother and son were well and truly at loggerheads. Alberto promised her to return to his studies (and he made an effort to do so) but fell short of completing his final exams. The attraction of the motorcycle was simply too great. On 28 June 1936, just short of his 18th birthday (he was born on 13 July 1918), Ascari entered the Sertum in a 24-hour regularity trial in northern Italy. This, his first competition, was marred by two tumbles – one on the road to the Cisa Pass and the other just after Pisa where rear-brake failure vaulted him over a public lavatory, startling several ladies therein, and into the soft loam of a tomato field. After repairs to machine and rider they scored a category win in a trial at Lario a week later, a satisfying and inspiring first success.

For the 1937 season Ascari organised a place with the Scuderia Automobilistica Ambrosiana, set up in November 1936 by four Milanese racers and named after the city's patron saint, Sant'Ambrogio. While mainly dedicated to car racing, the new *scuderia* or team also had a motorcycle chapter which acquired 500cc Gileras for the established Silvio Vailati and newcomer Ascari.

In gaining this coveted place Alberto's renowned surname was a clear advantage. It was an honour for the Scuderia Ambrosiana to have the son of the great Antonio on its books, an honour that also commanded good starting money. But Alberto showed that he was more than a mere ornament. In a dozen 1937 events he scored five victories, one at Forlì shared with his team, and finished second twice.

This did not fully occupy the young Ascari. In fact he regarded bike racing as his sport, a sport about which he was passionate but a sport nonetheless. Learning to drive on a Fiat Ballila, he gained his licence at 18 and was taking an active interest in the family business, which now represented Fiat in Milan. He was quite prepared to settle down to a car-selling career with the odd race as an enjoyable and stimulating – as well as promotionally beneficial – diversion.

His focus was changed by an offer in the spring of 1938 from another Milan resident, Bianchi. Tracing its origins to a bicycle workshop set up in Milan in 1885 by the eponymous Edoardo, Bianchi had become a prominent maker of cars, trucks and motorcycles as well as bicycles. And its racing motorcycles were stormers. Bianchi riders crossed the finishing line first in 95 races between 1925 and 1930. Wearing their blue and white kits were Tazio Nuvolari, then founding his legend, and Achille Varzi, his great car-racing career still ahead.

Bianchi was a brand to which a young Italian would-be racer could aspire in the 'thirties, as were Gilera and Moto Guzzi, but unlike Bianchi these firms were not sited smack dab in the city in which Alberto Ascari was born in his parent's house. And Bianchi liked what it saw in the attractive character of Ascari, now a handsome young man with a rich head of swept-back hair, piercing brown eyes and a ready smile. Offered a monthly retainer of 300 lire with prize-money bonuses, he accepted a place with Bianchi.

From 1938 into 1940 the yearly race schedule was shrinking as a result of Fascist Italy's exit from the League of Nations in December 1937 and her lack of domestic sources of petrol. Alberto raced 13 times for Bianchi in those years and returned a handsome tally of five victories. When he didn't win Ascari usually retired, matching the pattern he had set with the Ambrosiana team. Here was a man who set his sights on victory virtually whatever the costs.

In July 1939 Alberto Ascari turned 21. We may safely assume that under the terms of his father's will this brought a welcome bonus to his personal finances. His majority granted him, as well, a meagre but significant independence from the strictures of the *maresciallo*. The larger picture for all Italians, however, was troubling. In April Mussolini's troops crossed the Adriatic to occupy Albania and on 22 May the Italian government signed its 'Pact of Steel' with Hitler's Germany. When war broke out in September, Italy declared herself neutral. Nevertheless the storm clouds over Europe darkened Italy as well.

Against this turbulent backdrop Alberto Ascari explored his options for an entry into racing on four wheels instead of two. The competition calendar for 1940 offered numerous events, in most of which the German teams had committed to entries, including the Mille Miglia as well as single-seater races for 1,500cc cars. This promised lively competition between the Pact of Steel partners. Ascari intended to be represented in both categories.

For a sports car he turned to a friend and former colleague of his father, Enzo Ferrari. After severing his long-standing links with Alfa Romeo, Ferrari set up an engineering company in Modena. Ascari met with Ferrari. They discussed the rules of the Mille Miglia, set for nine laps of a fast 103-mile road circuit near Brescia on 28 April. The prize for a class victory was 10,000 lire. In addition, Fiat posted a prize of 5,000 lire for a win by a car that was a Fiat or at least Fiat-based. Could Ferrari build such a car for Ascari? Perhaps for the 1,500cc class? At a Christmas Eve dinner party only four months before the race, he agreed to give it a try.

They agreed on a price of 20,000 lire for Alberto's car, which meant that it couldn't be trimmed as lavishly as a sister '815' made for a wealthy Modenese marquis, Lotario Rangoni Machiavelli. To qualify for the Fiat prize the two roadsters were based on the chassis of the Fiat 508C Ballila and had straight-eight engines made up of many Fiat parts. Their open bodies were built by Carrozzeria Touring in Milan, not far from Ascari's home. Alberto stopped by to see them being made, just by chance, he said, 'but his curiosity, his anxiety to see the 815 completed, betrayed him,' a Touring man recalled. 'He looked, he touched, he questioned with the unmistakable passion which for him was only just beginning.'

These cars were created in secret by the cautious Ferrari and entered only provisionally just two weeks before the Mille Miglia. In the meantime Ascari saw to his single-seater needs. 'In the spring of 1940,' related racing driver Luigi 'Gigi' Villoresi, 'I was approached by a young man who wanted to buy an Alfa Romeo. I persuaded him that it would be better for him to buy a Maserati, a 1.5 litre 6-cylinder supercharged single-seater model, which I would let him have for 12,000 lire. He told me he could just about afford this figure because another racing driver, Piero Taruffi, had agreed to come in with him on the deal.'

Taruffi remembered the transaction with Ascari a bit differently: 'I had sold a half-share in my own 1938 Maserati to Alberto Ascari whom I had met through motorcycle events when he was riding a 350 for Bianchis. He was terribly keen, I knew, to get into the Gilera [motorcycle] team, but it was impossible at that time because there was no vacancy. However, as it was simply not in his temperament to wait, he offered to buy a half-share in my Maserati on the condition that he could drive it at Tripoli and in the Targa Florio.'

Thus Alberto became a partner in a two-year-old third-hand 6CM Maserati whose engine, Villoresi ruefully recalled, 'was still hot from welding!' On 10 March *l'Auto Italiana* announced that Alberto Ascari, 'son of the prematurely killed and unforgettable ace of the wheel,' would make his car-racing debut in the Targa Florio in May. As it had been since 1937, this was held on a road circuit in the Favorita Park on the western edge of Palermo, set in a rich valley between two mountain ranges.

Only in April did the news break that Ferrari was building a sports car to compete in the Mille Miglia's 1,500cc class against numerous Lancia Aprilias and that Ascari would drive one. Although he posed in his finished car with close friend Silvio Vailati at his side, the motorcyclist was seen as too excitable a partner for the heavy-footed Alberto. Instead he was accompanied by his cousin Giovanni Minozzi. Son of Antonio's sister Marianna, Minozzi had been 27 when he accompanied his uncle's casket on the sad journey from Montlhéry to Milan. He was delegated to exert a sobering influence.

After a haranguing by a Fascist-party official the Ascari 815, bearing number 66, was flagged away at 6:21am, a minute after Rangoni's sister car. Alberto, wearing a typical motorcyclist's sleeveless waistcoat over his jersey, soon overtook his team-mate and easily assumed the class lead. Minozzi had only praise for his daring, even heedless driving style but on the second lap one of the Fiat-made rocker arms failed and Ascari was out. Rangoni lasted longer in a car that had enjoyed more pre-race testing, but retired as well. Ferrari admitted in his memoirs that 'the car was not a success, mainly on account of the haste with which it had been constructed.' It was anything but a total loss for Ascari, however. In February 1943 he sold his 815 for the handsome sum of 42,000 lire.

Expecting Mercedes-Benz to return to the fast Tripoli circuit with the 1939 winners, its W165 models, Alfa Romeo had trained assiduously for the 12 May race with its Type 158. Maserati also turned out with a full works team. Against opposition of this quality young Alberto did well to qualify 12th fastest of 23 entrants and to finish ninth, two laps behind the leaders, in his outdated Maserati. Kitted out in pristine white coveralls, the driver was judged by *l'Auto Italiana* to have 'an easy style, controlled, free of tactics, deliberate – all qualities not easy to find in a young man like Ascari'.

Eleven days later, on a Thursday, he competed at Palermo in the Targa Florio. There he was less fortunate, running out of road and damaging his Maserati. On the Sunday Ascari went to Genoa for the motorcycle race that was destined to be the last motorsporting event before Italy entered the war on 10 June. Tragically, he witnessed there the fatal injury in a crash of his close friend Vailati. Neither his Targa retirement nor Vailati's death were warming memories of motorsport for Ascari to take into wartime.

In the meantime this interesting young man, well-to-do, well born and offering an appealing mixture of earnestness and daring, was attracting a coterie. Nine years older than Alberto, racing driver Gigi Villoresi had lost a younger brother in a testing crash in 1939. While not strictly a fraternal substitute, young Ascari became a close friend. Indeed, with one of Alberto's uncles they established a business that transported fuel and vehicles to North Africa, where Italy's possessions included Libya and Abyssinia. Because this transport was vital to Italy's war effort, Ascari was not called up.

Vivacious members of the Villoresi circle were the blonde Tavola sisters of Milan. In 1940 Gigi introduced Alberto to Maria Antonietta 'Mietta' Tavola, a year older than Ascari. Foxily appealing, Mietta became Alberto's girlfriend. They were wed on 22 January 1942 and their son Antonio was born on 2 August of the same year. They passed a quiet war, although one scare was the passage of German troops, who did not hesitate to attach eligible Italians to their forces. Alberto and others of his age hid in the woods for more than a week to escape their searches.

At war's end Ascari was a settled businessman, dedicating his efforts to a revival of the family car dealership. He put aside thoughts of racing because, as he said, he wanted his mother to have 'as peaceful an old age as possible'. Nor did Mietta encourage a resumption of his pre-war sport: 'When I met him, in 1940, I didn't know him as a driver, even though he had already had a few successes. And I hoped that the war would last forever (well, I don't really mean that), so that racing wouldn't start again.' But start again it did – without, however, Alberto Ascari.

Enjoying Mietta's good cooking, Alberto had taken on the rounded profile that won him the amiable nickname 'Ciccio' or 'chubby'. He was a type known as *'un uomo quadrato'* – literally a 'square' but in fact implying that he was sensible and level-headed. Too sensible to get back into racing, even as a pastime as it had been for him before the war? So it seemed. After 25 July 1946 he also had a daughter, Patrizia.

Meanwhile Gigi Villoresi and friends reawakened the Scuderia Ambrosiana and welcomed, with many successes, the revival of racing in 1946. Alberto went along to events to support his friend. Late that year, however, he sat at the controls of Gigi's 4CL Maser and, at Naples, tried it for a few laps during practice. 'There,' said Villoresi, 'immediately in evidence, was his innate ability to become a great race driver.' The quick laps had come easily. Ascari followed this with clandestine practice at Monza.

Early in 1947 Alberto Ascari received a treasured invitation. He was chosen to compete in a unique race series in Egypt. All drivers would pilot the same little 1,100cc Cisitalia single-seaters, drawn by lot from a pool of 22 identical cars. Three such events were scheduled. The first was on 9 March on Cairo's fast 1½-kilometre El Gézirah Park circuit on one of the four islands of the Nile River in the heart of Cairo. Ascari was invited as one of the *motociclisti* taking part, in contrast to the proper *piloti*. He was, as usual, 'son of the unforgettable ace Antonio Ascari' and at 28 was the youngest of the 16 drivers participating.

In the straitened circumstances of post-war Italy this 'Cisitalia Cruise' was a glamorous and exotic event, bankrolled by Cisitalia chief Piero Dusio. Refuelling at Lecce, two tri-motor transports flew the drivers and others to Cairo on the morning of 22 February. Fêted by King Farouk and Cairo society, the drivers toured the sights at Giza and at Alexandria, where one of the other two races was to be held.

The racing format was two 25-lap heats and a 50-lap final. The experienced Franco Cortese won the first heat. Second-heat winner was Piero Taruffi, who had done much of the development testing of the little Cisitalia. Behind him, however, was Ascari, thus easily qualifying for the final. This was started by none other than car-mad King Farouk himself.

In the final the two heat winners, followed by Cisitalia chief Dusio, were away ahead of Alberto. Taruffi led, setting the fastest lap, but retired. Ascari pressurised then passed Dusio and set his sights on the leading Cortese. There seemed every chance of catching him but at the finish Ascari fell 13 seconds short. It had been the most exciting drive of the race. 'Without gainsaying the merits of Cortese and Taruffi,' wrote *l'Auto Italiana*, 'the overwhelming final of Ascari had equal value and his second place had the decisive merit of a victory.'

A fellow competitor, Giovanni Lurani, pointed out that – contrary to the views of many – Ascari was not new to car racing and that his pre-war car outings 'had let us see the makings of a future ace'. The Cairo race, he said, 'confirmed the rosiest expectations and [his] very fast, courageous pursuit in the final is the guarantee that the Italian auto world can count on one champion more.'

The 'Cisitalia Cruise' returned to Italy, eschewing the other planned races. Spectator interest had been low. Neither did the circus carry on to Spain or South America as had been hoped. Alberto Ascari drove a Cisitalia only twice more, retiring in June at Rome's Caracalla circuit and placing fifth behind bigger cars at Albi in July. Never again would he race such a small car. He would, instead, be accepted at once into racing's highest echelons. But was this the life for *un uomo quadrato*?

Alberto Ascari is only six on 19 October 1924 when he poses at Monza with his father, left of the cockpit, and his Alfa Romeo P2. At the right is mechanic Giulio Ramponi while Enzo Ferrari beams from between Ascari father and son.

With the victorious Alfa at Monza in October 1924 (above) are Vittorio Jano, far left, and Nicola Romeo behind the radiator. Winner Antonio Ascari is behind the folded windscreen. In 1924 he leads the French Grand Prix (below) until his engine block fails just before the finish. Ramponi tries vainly to restart.

At the age of six Alberto is considered to be the 'mascot' for his father's success in the 1924 Italian Grand Prix (above left and right). He is held aloft as his father celebrates with

Nicola Romeo (bottom left). Antonio wins again in the Belgian Grand Prix on 28 June 1925 (bottom right). Four weeks later he is killed in the French Grand Prix.

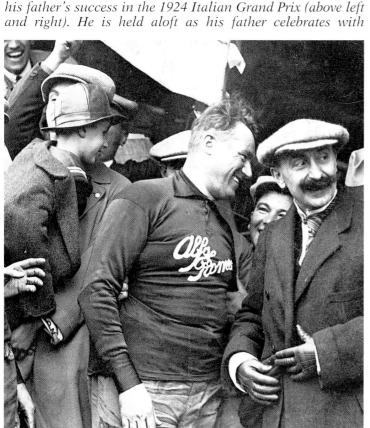

Hiding behind her sunglasses in a car driven by Gigi Villoresi's brother Emilio is the attractive Mietta Tavola, sitting next to her sister. Mietta does not yet know that she is destined to become the wife of Alberto Ascari. Ascari, meanwhile, is sharpening his competitive skills as a member of the Gilera motorcycle racing team.

Just after the completion of his new 815, built by a new company set up by Enzo Ferrari and bodied by Touring, Ascari poses in April 1940 with his friend and fellow motorcycle racer Silvio Vailati (above). Wearing driving gloves, Ascari strikes a solo pose (below). It is big news that the son of the great Antonio will race in the 1940 Mille Miglia.

CHAPTER 2

Reluctant racer

The world of motorcycle racing did not soon forget the many pre-war victories notched up by Alberto Ascari. He had shown decisive skill on two wheels. In 1946 Bianchi, struggling back from the 1943 bombing of its factories, began weighing the idea of building a new racing motorcycle. It would be made especially for Ascari, exploiting not only his skill but also his famous name. Such a machine would have raised the Bianchi profile to that of such race-mad rivals as Norton, Guzzi and Gilera. But boardroom conflicts killed off the project in 1947.

In the meantime the car-racing world had embraced its new star after his scintillating demonstration at Cairo. Close friend Gigi Villoresi, totally committed to racing as a career, was a lively, intelligent and convincing advocate of the merits of the sport. He was competing as a member of the revived Scuderia Ambrosiana, which reached out from Italy to form links with English racers. 'I will not dwell too deeply on how this set-up worked,'

Suitably kitted out, aspiring racing driver Alberto Ascari is photographed in a car he never raced, a 1935 Maserati 4CM 1500. Maseratis do provide his first serious competitive drives on four wheels.

wrote team mechanic 'Wilkie' Wilkinson, 'except to say that both Britain and Italy had severe exchange control regulations at the time, and some ingenuity was required to run any sort of international racing team.' Team members owned their individual cars and the Scuderia sorted out the entries and finances.

The Alfa Romeo 'Alfetta' was still the quickest 1½-litre supercharged Grand Prix car, but the works was keeping them for its own use. Neither before nor after the war could Ascari acquire one, with or without his historic links with the marque. Ferrari was known to be producing a GP car of his own, but it had not yet surfaced. The remaining option was the 4CLT Maserati, a fast and pretty four-cylinder racer. The only problem was the price: 5 million devalued lire. Ascari managed to find 3 million and the rest he pledged with IOUs to Maserati and friends, including the now-silver-haired Villoresi. He became a proud Maserati owner and member of the Ambrosiana team.

Alberto Ascari's first proper Grand Prix race under the new post-war regulations (his pre-war single-seater races had been in the *Voiturette* category) was on 6 July 1947 at Reims, France. If he was expecting an agreeable return to the top level of the sport on this fast road course in the champagne country, he was grievously disappointed. So were many other runners, for of 20 starters only seven finished, none of them Ambrosiana starters.

'The engine blew up,' said Ascari. 'Indeed, everything that could blow up blew up! For a time, still in debt to Maserati, I wasn't sure whether to go off and join the Foreign Legion or to strip down the Maserati piece by piece and rebuild it. I chose the second solution even though it seemed to me the *least* logical at the time.' He borrowed the car of another Scuderia member to race at Albi the following weekend, where he finished fifth.

His Maserati repaired, Ascari mounted it for a race on the Promenade des Anglais and gardens at Nice on the next weekend. While Villoresi roared off to a win, late in the race Alberto received a driving lesson from the great French champion Jean Pierre Wimille, at the wheel of a tiny blue Gordini. The two had a slam-bang set-to until Ascari, fighting misfiring and not yet schooled in the fine art of brake conservation, had to pit. He finished fourth.

Two more races in France in August produced mixed results for the Milanese newcomer, still referred to as 'the worthy son of the great champion'. The extremely fast circuit at Comminges was hit by a downpour that favoured the heavy Talbots and demoted Alberto to seventh place. A race on tortuous roads at Strasbourg was a complete contrast. There Ascari took the lead in a Grand Prix for the first time, only to be halted by a dropped valve. Villoresi saved the day with a win for Ambrosiana.

For his next race on 7 September Alberto Ascari could rest comfortably at home and make his way easily to the circuit. His smile was even broader than usual as he reflected that this 18th Grand Prix of Italy was being held over exactly the same roads in Milan where he had turned his first exciting laps of a big city square on Bassetti's motorcycle some two decades earlier. Monza was the rightful venue, but it hadn't yet been revived from its wartime condition.

The Milanese, packed into streets and stands for this greatest race of the year, saw what they expected – a victory for the home-town team of Alfa Romeo, making one of its rare 1947 appearances. Four Alfas started. For much of the early going Ascari showed a distinct lack of respect by challenging Consalvo Sanesi's Alfa for third place with his much-less-powerful Maserati. Urging him

on, the crowd seized on his nickname: '*Ciccio*! *Ciccio*!' Chubby or not, Alberto showed them some inspired race driving. A loose fuel-tank strap dropped him back but he still finished fifth, best of the rest behind the Alfas.

After this race Alberto was still 'worthy son of the great captain of the Alfa Romeo P2 squadron'. At Milan, however, wrote the respected Corrado Filippini, he was 'a model of thoughtful audacity, of beautiful style, of determination. This young driver is a revelation.' Ascari had acquired a new and influential fan in tall, experienced editor Filippini.

Two weeks later the Ambrosiana team-mates travelled to Lyon for the French Auto Club's Grand Prix, in which both their Maseratis retired. They were back in time for a sports-car race on the streets of Modena on 28 September. There the risks of racing round the houses were tragically revealed. When one car swerved to avoid another it veered into the crowd, causing many injuries and some deaths. The race was flagged to a stop and victory awarded to the man who was leading: Alberto Ascari, driving a new A6GCS Maserati. It was his first victory on four wheels, but not one that admitted of great celebration.

GP Maseratis were the weapons of choice for the Grand Prix run on the roads of Lausanne, Switzerland, on 5 October. There Ascari displayed the decisive style that would come to characterise his career. He was quickest in practice and first away at the start – jumping it in fact – and off to an early lead, setting the fastest lap. On the 14th lap, however, he had a fright and a half: 'At the bottom of a hill that tightened into a bend to be taken almost at a standstill, when I put my foot on the pedal I noticed there was no resistance: a small hydraulic pipe had broken. There's no use asking me how I got out of it, because I still don't know. I managed to change gear, skid to the limit and remain on the road. I sweated a few hours later when the race had finished, thinking back on the episode.' After a pit stop he retired.

Watching Ascari at Lausanne, Giovanni Lurani ventured a comment on his style: 'Although impetuous and determined, Ascari seems calm and equipped with an authoritarian style that will permit him to be the equal of his great parent, whom he recalls in his character and his desire to win. Ascari has only one defect which unfortunately needs healing! He's young, and when a certain exuberance is behind him our Alberto will find his place in the circle of aces.' A year later people would be saying similar things about a young Stirling Moss, who like Ascari was pressing on more sharply than some of his rivals preferred. Like Moss, Ascari did not suppress that 'exuberance' but rather made it an integral part of his equipment as a driver.

Alberto ended his season in a sports-car race on the streets of Turin. Ferrari's 2-litre V12 was getting into its stride, and with Frenchman Raymond Sommer at its wheel it had the legs of the Villoresi/Ascari A6GCS Maseratis. Alberto retired with a gearbox mainshaft breakage of this still-new model. When the points for the Italian championship were totted up at the end of the year Ascari was fifth behind leader Villoresi, Varzi, Trossi, and Sanesi. Within a year Trossi would be retired and Varzi would be dead, killed in a racing crash at Bremgarten. Opportunities were opening up for Italy's most talented young driver.

The cycle-winged sports Maserati was Ascari's mount for his first two 1948 races, the demanding Giro di Sicilia – literally a 620-mile lap of Sicily – and the Mille Miglia. He finished neither. The reasons why would contribute to a lifelong aversion to black cats, one of which scampered in front of his car on the way to the Sicilian start. 'First of all I left the road,' he recalled, 'fortunately without serious consequences. Then I burned out the "Delco" [generator]; then the rear axle broke. My mechanic fell ill and was sick. Finally, before I arrived at Palermo the car made a sudden leap and stopped. I opened the bonnet; a rag was caught around the engine!

'A month later,' Ascari continued, 'I was going toward the start for the Mille Miglia at Brescia when a large tomcat cut across my path. I was unsettled and left reluctantly. For a while we were in the lead. Then at Rimini it became difficult to change gear; the lever was stiff. To make it work I had to use both hands. Each time I had to change gear while coping with a dangerous stretch the manoeuvre became a nightmare. The mechanic and I were in despair. We pushed on somehow or other as far as Monsummano, but there a connecting-rod bearing melted and we had to retire.'

Is it any wonder that ever afterward black cats were anathema to Ascari? His friend Umberto Masetti related

one such experience: 'The two of us were going from Modena to Milan. We were in his car and, of course, he was driving. Suddenly, in the village of San Pancrazio, not far from Parma, a black cat crossed the road. I didn't see it, so I was surprised when Alberto braked heavily and parked on the right side of the road. "But what happened, Alberto?" I asked. "Are you unwell?" "A black cat crossed the road," he answered, and added, "Please take the wheel." I saw that his face was pale. We changed places.'

In Marseilles, related another friend, 'we were all forced to go on foot or in taxis because he refused to touch his Fiat 1400, our group's only car, until the end of the race – for five days, that is – because the morning after his arrival he had found a big black cat sleeping on its bonnet. Another occasion was a return trip from a race at Syracuse with Ascari sitting on his suitcases in the train's corridor because the sleeping compartment he shared with Villoresi was number 13 and that of me and Serafini was number 17. The situation was only resolved when, having explained the situation to the priest who occupied number 14, he kindly agreed to swap.'

For Grand Prix racing in 1948 'rising star' Ascari was still a member of the Scuderia Ambrosiana. The team maintained its close links with Maserati, of whom it was a customer, albeit one with a priority for mods and new models. Early in the year Ascari negotiated a deal with Maserati's Omer Orsi: 'I gave him my rebuilt GP Maserati in exchange for a brand-new flame-red model, to be ready in three months. In the meantime I felt it important to assure him that I would pay all the IOUs, from the first to the last, without asking for one day's postponement. Thus I remained without a car for three months so as to avoid the "Foreign Legion" alternative.'

Until his new car was ready Alberto borrowed another Maserati *monoposto* from the Ambrosiana stable to compete in the important Monte Carlo Grand Prix in May. At the principality his car lacked the two-stage superchargers that the others were sporting; he placed fifth after a stop for a plug change. Sports Maseratis were his rides for his next races at Bari and Mantua, stripped of their wings on both occasions to compete under the new 2-litre Formula 2. Misfiring from the start, Ascari's mount didn't improve with fresh plugs at Bari and retired.

The race at Mantua on 13 June was rich with nostalgic resonance. Staged in Tazio Nuvolari's home town with the help of members of his family, it was an enthusiastic tribute to his great racing career. At 56, piloting a Ferrari 166, Nuvolari charged away from the start in his usual pyrotechnic style. Right with him, in the first laps, was Alberto Ascari. The two Italian racing generations were never in closer contact. Tazio's health was not good enough for him to last many laps and Alberto – nicknamed 'Berto' by one magazine – fell to fifth after brake troubles and a wheel change.

After Mantua the new flame-red Maserati racer was ready for the race on San Remo's Ospedaletti road circuit on 27 June. And it was a dilly. For the Orsis Alberto Massimino had designed a new low and light chassis for the supercharged 16-valve four-cylinder Maser motor with its 260 alcohol-fed horsepower. Two of the new models, the 4CLT/48, were ready for Ascari and Villoresi. They would debut it on a course so tight – one writer called it a 'microscopic Nürburgring' – that the winning average speed would not exceed 60mph.

Before the race, wrote Luciano Palomba, 'Alberto appeared calm and in a good mood as usual. He felt that luck was on his side that day. Villoresi looked at him, amazed by his calm. "Are you ready to do battle?" He seemed to ask. Alberto did not reply, avoided his friend's eyes, got into the car, set off and got to the front immediately.' They won one-two. But this time instead of Gigi leading, as had so often been the case, Alberto took the early command and held it to the finish in a race of just over three hours. Villoresi was second after two pit stops.

It was, at long last, 'the first important and complete victory of Alberto Ascari' as Corrado Millanta wrote. He remembered the quiet newcomer who had stood in apparent awe of the famous drivers before the trip to Cairo a year ago: 'He was sympathetic in aspect, a face radiating intelligence, seriousness and good will. New to this environment, he spoke little and listened closely to all.' Ascari had listened – and learned.

Although the opposition comprised older Maseratis and Talbots, in the field were Nino Farina, Prince Bira, Raymond Sommer, and Louis Chiron – none a pushover. And the winning Maserati's cockpit was scattered with stones from the deteriorating road surface. 'In any case,' wrote Millanta after San Remo, 'one thing's for sure and

that's that – as 23 years ago – we again have the joy of shouting the name "Ascari" during the development of a race with the conviction of desiring, counting on and standing up for the victory of an authentic ace.' Alberto was still Antonio's son. But he was beginning to be recognised for his own merits.

The first encounter between the new Maserati and the Type 158 Alfa Romeo came only a week later at Switzerland's demanding Berne circuit in the Grand Prix of Europe. Better though they were, the Maseratis couldn't cope with the more powerful Alfettas. Nevertheless Villoresi succeeded in placing his third ahead of Sanesi's Alfa. Ascari had been running fourth but fell behind Sanesi after making a late-race pit stop. It was a sombre weekend in which a crowded programme and an oily circuit had taken the lives of one motorcyclist and two racing drivers.

The death of Achille Varzi at Berne was the proximate motive for the invitation extended by Alfa Romeo to Alberto Ascari to step into the cockpit of one of its three cars for the French Grand Prix at Reims on 18 July. Ascari accepted, shrugging off Villoresi's protestations that he should remain loyal to their new Maseratis, now nicknamed 'San Remo' after Alberto's victory. At Reims he had no difficulty in outpacing Sanesi, Alfa's works tester. Against Jean Pierre Wimille, acknowledged the fastest driver of the day and indeed among the best of all time, his fastest race lap was only 1.6 seconds slower than the Frenchman's best of 2:41.2.

In the 311-mile Grand Prix Wimille and Ascari easily moved to the front. Extra stops for Wimille meant that Ascari held the lead for some laps but after the main refuelling stops the Alfa management signalled its drivers to resume their assigned positions, which meant that in the race's final laps Alberto had to let Sanesi pass him into second place. He finished third a half-second behind. This was not, perhaps, the kindest courtesy that could have been afforded to the son of Alfa's great Antonio in what turned out to be Alberto's one and only race for Alfa, in the same event – albeit at a different circuit – in which his father was killed 23 years earlier.

In August and September of 1948 Alberto had three more races for Maserati in their A6GCS sports-racer. The first was at Pescara, a 17-mile circuit with two fast stretches. Maserati fielded three cars for him, Villoresi and Giovanni Bracco, who relished tighter tracks and hillclimbs. The Ferraris were present too, and they led the early laps under the hot August sun. On the third of 18 laps Alberto limped into the pits with a broken leaf-spring attachment. He retired, wrote Millanta, 'to the great disappointment of a public who by now knew, appreciated and followed with great sympathy this, our young champion with the glorious name.'

Astonishingly, the Maserati pits were also visited by Giovanni Bracco. Nothing was wrong with his car, he said. He just couldn't stand the 'infernal pace' of the long straights! He offered his car to Maserati tester Guerrino Bertocchi, who was not slow to install Ascari in it instead. By the fourth lap Alberto was third behind a Ferrari and Maserati, maintaining a quick yet steady gait. Both of them obliged him by retiring.

Undeterred by a hectic pit stop that almost set his car alight, he seized the lead. During the last lap but one Ascari grinned, gestured and shouted to a photographer friend. The normally-placid Milanese knew that he had scored an important victory for Maserati against Ferrari in a race of almost four hours – and he was relishing it! His other two sports-car races for Maserati, at Naples and Florence, were anticlimactic. He set the fastest lap in the former but retired in both.

In a season weighted toward the final months Ascari had four more Grand Prix races to contest in September and October of 1948. The first, on the streets of Turin, was the all-important GP of Italy, as usual with a full complement of Alfa Romeos and also with the first appearance of three Formula 1 Ferraris. The race was run in dire weather as Rodney Walkerley reported for *The Motor*: 'The rain poured monotonously down; the awnings of the stand sagged; the flags drooped miserably; the road was covered with deep pools through which the racing cars charged as if through water splashes, almost hidden as they went.

'Ascari,' continued Walkerley, 'driving with great calmness and very fast – obviously a coming man – stopped 50 seconds for plugs [after 11 laps] and fell back to twelfth place, such was the speed of the race.' By the finish he had clawed his way back to fourth. 'Optimum, and yet reaching both the highs and lows, was the race of Alberto Ascari, who has confirmed all his promise,' judged Corrado Filippini. 'Only one point with which to

burden Ascari: he drove three quarters of the race with neither goggles nor visor, something inconceivable for a driver who aspires to great achievements.'

No Ferraris or Alfas troubled the Ambrosiana aces in the British Grand Prix at Silverstone. There Ascari was reunited with Giulio Ramponi, his father's riding mechanic, who had settled in England in the 1930s. 'We had two Italian visitors in Villoresi and Ascari,' wrote Rodney Walkerley, 'who drove night and day to reach the circuit with their Type 4CLT/48 Maseratis, arriving just in time for four laps of unofficial practice – in which Ascari made fastest lap of any competitor. The two Italians took their back seat on the starting grid with great good humour.'

By the third of the 65 laps they were in the lead, an achievement which, said *l'Auto Italiana*, 'even excited the phlegmatic British sports fans' of whom 120,000 thronged the circuit. Walkerley: 'Both Ascari and Villoresi stopped twice for fuel during the race. During his first pit stop Ascari also changed both rear wheels for a pit stop lasting one and one half minutes. This effectively lost him the lead.' He placed second a quarter-minute behind.

At the banquet given that evening by the British Racing Drivers Club Alberto charmed the guests with his remarks in French, pausing frequently to ask his neighbours, Villoresi and Ramponi, 'How do you say that in French?' The English liked Alberto Ascari, and the feeling was mutual. 'Driving back towards Italy,' wrote Kevin Desmond, the driver decided that 'he rather liked the friendliness of the English, their way of life and their beautiful countryside. In the years to come, the English came to admire Alberto Ascari almost as much as his native Italians.'

In October Italy celebrated the reopening of the historic circuit at Monza with a full-scale Grand Prix. For the grand parade that preceded the race to hail the track's rebirth, Tazio Nuvolari was an honoured guest. Nuvolari made his feelings known when, on arriving at Monza with his wife, he went directly to shake the hand of Ascari. He clearly and publicly expressed his respect for the best of Italy's new generation of drivers.

The race was a command performance for all the current competitors. Alfa Romeo entered four cars. Could anyone make a dent in their all-conquering phalanx? Ferrari-mounted Sommer made a gallant early try but was out in a handful of laps. In another Ferrari Nino Farina challenged Piero Taruffi in the fourth Alfa but also fell by the wayside. Behind the Alfas it was destined to be Alberto Ascari in fifth place, outlasting other rivals to finish 'best in class'. In Spain two weeks later a good chance was lost when his Maserati's induction pipe failed after only one lap. The win went to teammate Villoresi.

By now the Villoresi/Ascari duo or *binomio*, as the Italians say, was well established. They had raced the same cars for the same teams through much of 1947 and all of 1948. In the GP at Monza their best laps differed by only a fifth of a second – to Villoresi's advantage. The two men had known each other for a decade and had been business partners as well as team members. They were often referred to by the press as 'teacher' and 'pupil'. But was that their relationship? Villoresi begged to differ:

'Many say I was his master. It is not true: Alberto was a self-made driver. His style was enthralling, similar to that of the great Pietro Bordino, but even purer and more striking. He had the clarity and presence of mind of Varzi, but the fighting spirit of Nuvolari on the track. It was especially true at that time, as on first impression we did not understand each other and it would have been impossible for me to teach him anything.'

This did not mean that they did not co-operate, Villoresi added. 'One can have the gift, but one learns skill by racing. Take cornering, where one turn requires you to take an angle of incidence different from another turn. One is not so much interested in entering a turn fast, but in *leaving* it fast. When we were practising for a race he placed himself behind me to see how I positioned myself for the corners. Such things I taught to Alberto – respect for the engine, its machinery. Often we chatted and exchanged just about every idea that can be exchanged.'

Mechanic Pasquale Cassani was a fly on the wall for some of their dialogues: 'Ascari used to pay careful attention to everything Villoresi said. Sometimes Villoresi gave him advice spontaneously; on other occasions Ascari asked his colleague and great friend for advice. Between one test session and another their main subject was always the same: how to go faster, how to go through the bends of a circuit following the fastest line.

But they were also studying how to use the gears: "There you should use second gear." "No, I think third is better." "Perhaps you could take it in your stride but there's a risk: a minor error or uncertainty and you'll spin or go straight off," and so forth. At first Ascari often told Villoresi he was right. Later came the time when it was Ascari's turn to advise Villoresi, but by then it was very difficult for Gigi to keep pace with Alberto.'

Villoresi witnessed the transformation in his friend: 'When he put those goggles over his eyes they suddenly became as cold as steel, intense, concentrated. They were no longer the eyes of the "Ciccio" Ascari of minutes before. He had entered into the life of that race, and everything that the race represented. Up to the starter's flag we were the greatest friends in the world, each with his scruples as regards the other. But during the race each of us did everything in his power to beat the other. Whoever won did so because he had performed better.

'We always did things for ourselves, *not* for the public,' Villoresi added. 'We raced for private pleasures and sensations, but always with a sense of responsibility to whoever had put his cars at our disposal, even if this responsibility was not always reciprocated. Our principle was that whoever was in the lead after 40 laps of a 50-lap race must be left alone. We did this because it was stupid to flog the two cars; better to respect them.'

Giovanni Lurani turned to the classics to express the style and substance of their relationship: 'What a splendid example of a modern Damon and Pithias, the irreproachable, true and lively friendship between Gigi Villoresi and Alberto Ascari, firstly with Gigi as affectionate and knowledgeable master, then faithful partner in victories beside the younger and stronger pupil, who became Giotto inspired by his contemporary Cimabue.'

Ascari acknowledges a signal on his way to victory at Pescara on 15 August 1948. His stylish and consistent drive in a sports Maserati wins both the approval and the attention of the Ferrari team manager.

Alberto Ascari's first car-racing victory is scored on 28 September 1947 on the streets of Modena, home town of his Maserati.

At the start Ascari (24) is sandwiched between two Ferraris. He is leading when the race is stopped after spectators are killed when a car leaves the road.

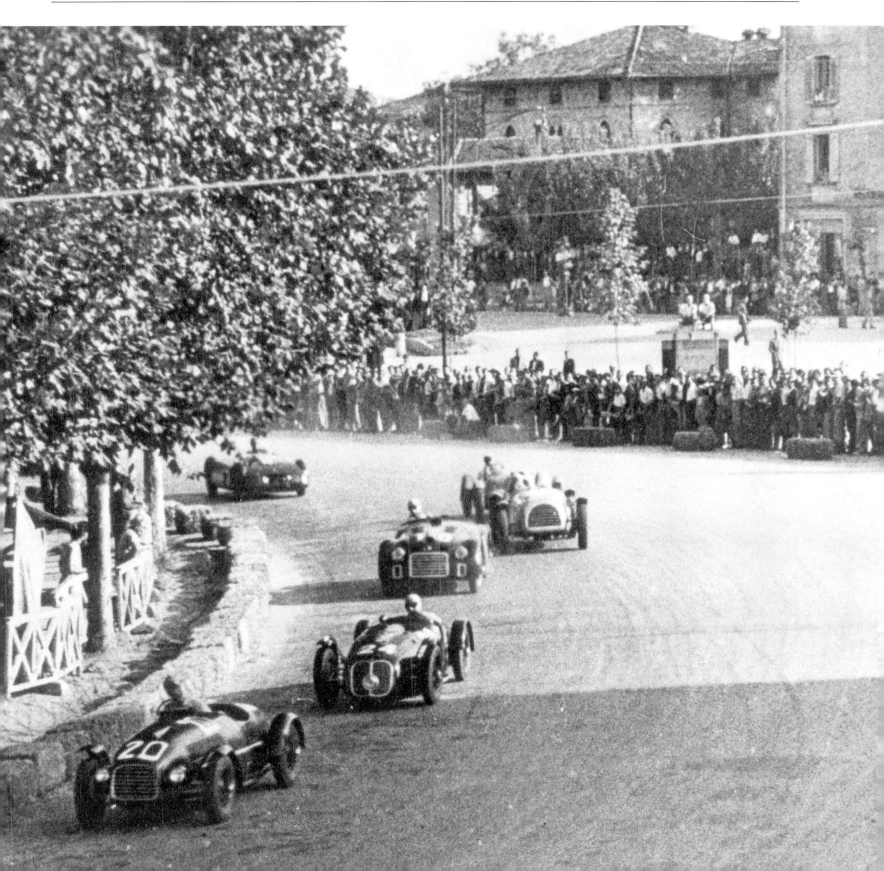

Without its lights and wings the A6GCS Maserati also competes in Formula 2 races, as at Mantua on 13 June 1948. Alberto (50) is fifth after a pit stop. His 1948 victory at Pescara (8) benefits from the retirements of Villoresi and Sommer. At Turin in October 1947 (34) he is leading team-mate Villoresi. He retires with gearbox problems in the still-new Maserati.

The Grand Prix 4CL Maserati is Ascari's mount for the Grand Prix of Comminges in August 1947 (24), the Grand Prix of Italy at Milan in September of the same year (34) and the 1947 Grand Prix of France at Lyon (44), in which he retires in spite of the best efforts of the mechanics of the Scuderia Ambrosiana (opposite).

Ascari gives the new 4CLT/48 Maserati a victory in its first race at San Remo on 27 June 1948 (opposite top), swinging inside Prince Bira on the gravel-strewn circuit. He races the same model successfully in Argentina in January 1949 (opposite bottom). Above, clockwise from top left: Ascari prepares to test a Maserati prototype in 1947, has his nose

attended to by Gigi Villoresi, reflects in the cockpit of one of the sports Maseratis, and prepares for the start at San Remo in 1948. Ascari has only one chance to race the marque that his father made famous, driving an Alfa Romeo 158 in the 1948 French Grand Prix (overleaf). He finishes third under team orders.

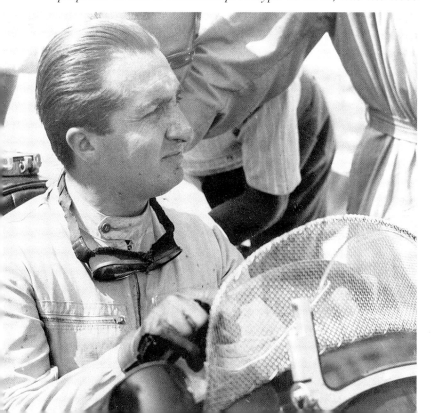

CHAPTER 3

Prancing horseman

The 1949 racing season began on 23 December 1948 when, sounding her mournful whistle, the ship *Italia* made speed from the port of Genoa bound for Buenos Aires. In her hold were ten racing cars for both Italian and Argentine drivers to use in the series of South American midsummer races known as the *Temporada*, which simply means 'season'. In this, the third year in which an Italian 'team' had made the journey, the drivers flew from Rome on 15 January. Among them, for the first time, was Alberto Ascari. He and Villoresi would drive 4CLT/48 Maseratis.

The first race on 30 January was marred by the death in a practice crash of France's great Jean Pierre Wimille. It was won outright by Ascari, who trounced all the local champions including their beloved Juan Fangio. 'When I succeeded in beating Fangio, I was really scared,' Alberto recalled. 'Half a million spectators were watching the race and I knew I wasn't their favourite. As I approached the finish line a crowd of people surged

At Berne on 3 July 1949 Alberto Ascari scores an historic first Formula 1 victory for Ferrari. Although the Alfas are absent it is a convincing triumph over a field that includes Nino Farina's Maserati.

toward me. I had never seen anything like it! I thought they wanted to lynch me.

'As soon as I crossed the line,' said Ascari, 'I jumped out of the car, ran into one of the garages, jumped over a fence and crossed one, two, three tennis courts at such a speed you'd have thought I was still in the racing car. The crowd followed me shouting. I hid in a car and stayed there for a good quarter-hour. Quite a lot of time passed before I realised that they only wanted to put me on their shoulders and carry me in triumph!'

The next two races in Buenos Aires and Rosario were wet ones. Alberto was leading at BA when a fractured exhaust pipe threatened to set his car alight, forcing his retirement just before the finish. He placed third at Rosario, where Farina won. The final race in Argentina was at Mar del Plata. There, recalled journalist Giovanni Canestrini, such was the intensity of emotion over the races that 'several young Italian workers came to plead with the drivers to make every possible effort to win. If they didn't win, they maintained, they would be forced to leave the city and, of course, their employment.' In the event they had to suffer a victory by Fangio; Ascari's Maserati was bedevilled by several pit stops.

The travelling circus next went to Brazil, where

Alberto was fourth at Interlagos – forerunner of the modern GP circuit. The next Sunday, 27 March, they competed at Rio de Janeiro on the Gavea circuit, so vicious it was known as 'the devil's trampoline'. 'I'd never raced in such conditions before,' admitted Ascari. 'Most of the track winds across old cobbled roads where barely two cars can pass at the same time. While I was trying out my car I found myself face to face with a bus that – for reasons unknown to me – was on the track. The day of the race, the police had to stop people from throwing themselves under my car to let Fangio win.

'Two laps after the start a Brazilian driver – unintentionally I'm sure – took a bend very wide while I was overtaking. This forced me to swerve, ending up against a wall. The car was going so fast that I continued the race in a field and ended up against a tree. I flew out of the car and landed on my head a short distance away from the fuel tank. And fainted. Unconscious, I inhaled the exhaust fumes from my car. When I awoke I found myself aboard another very fast-moving vehicle, this time an ambulance taking me to the hospital. I had broken my collarbone, three ribs and lost three teeth.'

While Alberto was convalescing in April and May, Juan Fangio had come to Europe and was winning at San Remo (where he had seen Ascari win the year before), Pau, Perpignan and Marseilles. This was unwelcome news to an attractive Milanese lady, Mietta Ascari: 'When I began to hear people talking about "Fangio" coming over from Argentina, I was afraid. I was afraid of this foreigner, and that Alberto was going to have to take many more risks just to overtake him. It's not easy being a driver's wife. You can't imagine what it's like living every hour of every day worrying whether he'll return. The main conversation in the family was: "When are you going to stop?"' Alberto's first serious crash had done nothing to lessen those tensions.

For his own European season Alberto Ascari might well have had the option of a seat in an Alfa Romeo 'Alfetta'. At Monza the previous autumn Alfa's chief, Ing. Gallo, had fixed his thick spectacles on Ascari and said, 'He's a driver whom I should very much like to have.' But busy with its new models and bereft of drivers after the death of Wimille, Alfa decided to sit out the 1949 season. Maserati would continue much as before, relying on private teams and owners while it developed its A6

production model. In fact it closed its Modena works from February to June of 1949 to retool its facilities.

Ferrari was the new power in the land. In the hands of the tigerish Sommer and the stylish Farina its 12-cylinder cars had shown impressive pace, albeit more from power than from handling. An ambitious new four-cam two-stage-supercharged Formula 1 car, the GP49, was under construction for 1949, a car that would deserve the most skilled drivers if Ferrari was, eventually, to challenge Alfa Romeo. Would Ascari be such a driver?

The historical connection was clear, as Ferrari's former secretary Romolo Tavoni explained: 'Ferrari had been a great friend of Alberto's father. Moreover he owed his entry into the Alfa Romeo racing team to Antonio and he hadn't forgotten it. Enzo was also a friend of Elisa, Antonio's widow, who was well aware that she couldn't resist her son's racing ambition. She used to speak to Enzo in these terms: "If you would test him at the wheel of a poor car, he would probably fall out of love with racing and I could feel more serene."'

The Ascari–Ferrari link was no secret to those outside the walls of the Maranello factory; as early as 1947 the Italian press was speculating that Ascari might drive a Ferrari car. At the tracks Ferrari's racing director Federico Giberti kept a close eye on the progress of the newcomer with the famous name. From the black-cat-jinxed Giro di Sicilia of 1948 Giberti reported to Ferrari that Ascari's driving was 'dangerous, showing excessive impetuosity and therefore not conserving the mechanical equipment, a trait needed for long circuits of this kind.' Neither did he consider Villoresi to be well suited to such events.

After watching Alberto win with the new Maserati at San Remo, however, Giberti was ready to proffer praise. He called his race 'optimum and consistent' and said that 'Ascari fully merited his success'. This, moreover, was a success with a proper Grand Prix car that showed that Ascari was on the brink of being ready for the Big Time. After his plucky victory at Pescara in August Ascari received an offer of employment from Ferrari but temporised by saying 'Thank you for your esteem, but I cannot leave Maserati, which has always helped me.'

Enzo Ferrari valued Ascari's skills but felt that the driver might be getting too good too soon, so much so that he might not be as malleable a motorist as Ferrari preferred. 'That boy gives himself too many airs,' he complained to Felice Bonetto when that driver recommended Alberto. But he respected Bonetto's endorsement. Neither was the position with Villoresi very clear. Gigi felt that Ferrari had dealt shabbily with the aftermath of his brother's fatal pre-war crash when testing a Scuderia Ferrari Alfa. And it was now clear that Ascari and Villoresi were a package deal.

As a friend of all parties, Corrado Filippini played a key role in reconciling drivers with team owner. Villoresi made his own peace with Ferrari. 'It is well known that Alberto arrived at Maranello with his great friend Villoresi, but he didn't need any introduction,' Romolo Tavoni recalled. 'Ferrari perfectly understood that he was a rising talent and bet on that horse without a sign of concern. Acting as Ascari's agent was journalist Corrado Filippini, thanks to whom Alberto could sign a real contract, detailed and punctilious, the first real contract that Ferrari was willing to sign with a driver after many years of simple letters or even simpler agreements by word of mouth and a handshake: this is the car, that is the race, we'll go 50–50 with start and prize money.'

Both Villoresi and Ascari were covered by the contracts, signed on 27 May, which treated them equally. They received monthly stipends of 100,000 lire and were entitled to half of all starting and prize money. 'From 1949 onwards Ferrari obviously held Ascari in higher esteem than Villoresi,' Tavoni said, 'because the former not only was faster but to his eyes appeared to be the present and the future, while the latter represented the past.'

The appointments were important to one man in particular, Ferrari engineer Aurelio Lampredi: 'Ferrari decided to take on two official works drivers – a fairly well-known quantity called Villoresi and a lesser-known driver, the same age as me, called Ascari. I soon struck up a friendship with both men, especially Alberto.' In fact Lampredi was a year older than Ascari, as they noted when they found that the engineer was born on the same date, 16 June 1917, as Mietta Ascari. 'We certainly enjoyed some fabulous birthday dinners on that day!' Lampredi recalled.

Lampredi too was a man of the future, for the Ferraris racing in 1949 were still the work of older engineer Gioachino Colombo. In the 2-litre Formula 2 they were V12-engined cars, the 166C. The new team's baptism was on 12 June 1949 in an F2 race at Bari on the Adriatic at Italy's 'ankle', where they could test the cars on a semi-closed circuit two days before the race. Finding that they were reaching peak revs, 6,800rpm, 300 metres before the ends of the straights, they decided to raise the final-drive ratios. In a race long enough to require refuelling Ascari took the lead at half-distance and won, setting a new lap record. As a debut drive it could hardly have been improved.

Two Formula 1 Ferraris, the existing 125C models, were taken to Spa for the Belgian GP a week later. For this race the two cars were set up in a manner that would become typical of Ascari, said team mechanic Pasquale Cassani: 'The key to his success was his way of going through the bends so that he could come out of them with his engine revving at some 100 or 200rpm higher than the others. For that reason, sometimes – depending on the circuit layout – he asked us to equip his car with a slightly shorter final gear ratio. This enabled him to accelerate more rapidly when exiting the bends.' For Spa the ratios of the two cars were 3.00:1 for Villoresi and 3.27 for Ascari; the latter is 'shorter'.

This alone was not the whole story, Cassani explained: 'Obviously, to obtain that result it wasn't sufficient to have such a modification of the gear ratio; everybody could have done it. In fact, not everybody could approach and go through the bends as he did, following a line so neat, precise and therefore fast.' The tactic didn't quite succeed for Ascari at Spa, where he had to give best to Villoresi. Stops for fresh tyres delayed the Ferraris to second and third behind the big trundling unsupercharged Talbot of Louis Rosier, who went through non-stop.

Ferrari kept his new drivers busy. Their next race was the following weekend, a Formula 2 contest at Monza. Ascari led through much of the race but was dropped to third at the finish by a balky gearbox. A week later, for the Swiss GP at Berne on 3 July, he and Villoresi arrived late on Friday evening. 'A series of incredible setbacks delayed the preparation of the cars,' said engineer Colombo. Saturday practice was bedevilled by problems with water in the supercharged engine's oil, dimming their prospects for the Sunday.

Team strategy was to start Alberto as the 'hare' with only 127 litres of fuel, while Villoresi carried 172 litres and hoped to run through non-stop. Ascari blitzed the start and by the fifth lap had opened up a 16-second lead over Gigi. The latter's plan was scuppered by his car's failure to pick up all its fuel, so he had to stop after all. Nevertheless they finished one–two on the demanding Berne road circuit, Ascari giving Ferrari its first major international Grand Prix victory.

Ascari had his own back on Fangio in their next Formula 2 encounter at Reims in the curtain-raising race for the French GP, in which the F1 Ferraris non-started. This time it was Fangio's turn to lead until sidelined by a gear-lever failure, leaving the victory to Ascari, who had been struggling with grabbing front brakes.

The last day of July found the GP circus at Holland's new circuit at the seaside resort town of Zandvoort for the first major Formula 1 event to be held there. Staged in two heats and a final, it saw a win for Villoresi in the first heat. Ascari, who had set fastest practice time, led in his wet and windy heat until his engine showed signs of distress, banging sharply on the overrun. He finished second. Before the final there was time to replace the supercharger, which was found to have a cracked housing.

Alberto easily led in the Dutch final, which was mercifully less damp. Six laps from the finish, Rodney Walkerley reported, he 'was mildly surprised to see a front wheel detach itself and found himself at an angle on the road one moment, into the soft sand the next, and himself a spectator from then on.' Gigi came to the rescue by winning for Ferrari. That the new man's style was still evolving was noted by Walkerley: 'One has to admit that Ascari seems to do far more driving than Villoresi at the same speed on the same corners.'

The next race, three weeks later, also featured the two-heats-and-a-final format. At England's Silverstone the *Daily Express* newspaper won friends by promoting an International Trophy race that attracted Ferrari. The usual two drivers settled for second in their respective heats. For the final it was warm; Ascari drenched his blue cloth helmet with water before donning it. He led from the start, at first ahead of Gigi and then from a grimly challenging Nino Farina's Maserati. Heat-winner Farina challenged Ascari on a few corners of the airfield circuit

but the latter fended him off to win the hour-long final.

Giberti's report to Ferrari on the race gave high marks to Alberto's performance: 'Ascari extremely capable, especially in the final. Followed continually by Farina, chased hard, he manoeuvred brilliantly to keep his first place.' Farina had his revenge the following weekend at Lausanne, taking the victory while Ascari was slowed by plug problems and a mischievous left front brake. The braking excitement provided by Lausanne in 1947 was not so easily forgotten.

Next on the agenda: the first proper post-war Grand Prix of Italy at Monza, which in 1949 was also accorded the distinction of being the European Grand Prix – then a peripatetic honour. Talbot and Maserati were expected, of course, as was a modified Maserati from the Scuderia Milan with Farina at the wheel. Nor could Alfa Romeo be excluded, as Colombo recalled: 'Even though the Milan firm had decided to retire from the races of that season, there were still rumours that that it might be making an exception for the Monza race.'

Ferrari's plans were laid accordingly. The existing 125C had been improved during the season and the GP49 was ready – or was it? This was a much more complex and ambitious car. It was tested at Monza, unpainted, two weeks before the GP. On the Friday before the race Ascari practised in a 125C, then on the Saturday in the new GP49, hastily returned from Maranello after modifications. They decided to race the new car. Alfa did not enter after all and Alberto and Gigi set the fastest and next-fastest qualifying times with them respectively.

The 313-mile race was Ascari's from start to finish. Among the 80 laps he stopped on the 28th and 55th, on the first stop substituting a new plug for one on which the electrode had broken. Behind him the opposition melted away, letting him moderate his speed toward the end. Neither his fastest lap (set on his second) nor his race average equalled Alfa's 1948 speeds, but then Alfa was not present. His GP49 Ferrari was a delicate beast, so much so that Lampredi said that just driving it out of the garage would make it boil. Ascari had taken the precaution of soaking his driving plimsolls (and doubtless his cloth helmet as well) in water before the race.

'I would like to place on record my admiration for Ascari's drive,' wrote Rodney Walkerley, 'his float through the fast curves with practised ease and perfect timing was a lesson remarkable in a driver of such comparatively brief experience.' The Italian press was more extravagant in its praise. The victory remained one that Ascari deeply treasured, and for good reason: 'Many thought my career was made easier by the fact my father was a champion. Instead it was a responsibility. I knew how good my father was and therefore I felt I had to live up to his reputation. Well, during that race I believed I would have made him happy by winning. So I did my best. I felt worthy of him when I won.'

Alberto Ascari ended a successful European season as Italian champion, this time ahead of Villoresi and Farina. Among both his public and his peers the standing of 'Ciccio' was confirmed. Looking back on 1949 Rodney Walkerley wrote that 'Alberto Ascari, who began Grand Prix driving only in 1947, strode through to stardom last season, proving himself to be extremely fast, unspectacular to those who did not look very closely at what was being done at the wheel, very cool and very steady – traits he may have learnt from his friend Villoresi, who also specialises in not going off the road, although travelling faster than he appears.'

Their next means of travel was considerably slower than that to which they were accustomed: the steamship *Conte Grande*. She slipped her moorings at Genoa in mid-November bound for Buenos Aires with an even larger complement of cars than the year before: six Ferraris, 15 Maseratis, two Talbots, and two Alfa Romeos. One of the Ferraris, a 166 Barchetta, was specially painted in the Argentine colours of blue and yellow as a gift to Evita Duarte Perón.

Much larger as well, the complement of drivers to compete in the *Temporada* races included a new recruit to the Ferrari strength, former motorcycle champion Dorino Serafini. His appointment came so late that he had only two days to organise the black-tie kit that was desirable, for the drivers naturally dined at the captain's table. Games of shuffleboard and more exotic entertainments kept tedium at bay during the 13-day voyage.

The 1950 Argentine season began a week before Christmas 1949 with a 109-mile race for General Perón's trophy. From a front-row starting position decided by a preceding sprint race, Alberto Ascari won convincingly in spite of searing heat, driving a supercharged 2-litre Ferrari V12. This time when he was mobbed after the race in Palermo Park he realised that the enthusiastic fans had only the best intentions. The passage of Christmas itself was made all the more cheering by the arrival at the Sheraton in Buenos Aires of a 'gigantic' *panettone* – a variety of seasonal cake – shipped from Italy by Villoresi's sister. Even in Argentina's heat the Milanese Christmas traditions were observed.

A week after New Year's the racers reconvened at Palermo Park to decide the holder of Evita Perón's cup. Villoresi won that honour after Ascari spun out of contention soon after the start. Uncharacteristically, he seemed to have taken the start in an irritated state of mind after a set-to with the team over some damage to the car's radiator.

On the following weekend in the race at Mar del Plata Ascari took the lead with Villoresi and Fangio jockeying right behind him. Gigi felt that Fangio was being overly obstructive of his efforts to pass, so he forced the issue and both drivers left the track to retire. This left the way clear for Alberto to win, an outcome which the Argentine press hotly criticised, saying that Villoresi deliberately knocked their favourite out of the race.

In this bitter atmosphere the fourth and final *Temporada* race was held at Rosario. Villoresi was the winner after newspaper – perhaps one of those so polemic against the Italian invaders – clogged Ascari's radiator grille and caused overheating that retired his Ferrari. After Rosario a 'reconciliation dinner' was organised for all the participants to show that there were no hard feelings after the Mar del Plata controversy.

The Ferrari team still had funds lodged in Brazil from the previous year's races, so Corrado Filippini organised a flight to Rio de Janeiro and rooms overlooking Copacabana Beach, where the drivers could enjoy the pleasures of the city's fabled carnival. From there the racers flew to Rome, where a youthful Giulio Andreotti extended the compliments of the government on their achievements and showed them around the Chamber of Deputies. The journey concluded with an audience with Pope Pius XII; several wives including Mietta joined the drivers for this honour.

Alberto Ascari returned to a European season for which Enzo Ferrari had developed a shrewd strategy. Alfa Romeo was expected back in Formula 1 to compete in the first year of the new drivers' World Championship. As before, it would be a formidable competitor. What had the Italians done in the 1930s when faced with the massed might of the German teams? They had turned to the secondary *Voiturette* formula, where they enjoyed great success. Well remembering these years, Enzo Ferrari planned the same for his team in 1950.

As Ferrari was well aware, race organisers had the same idea. Able as they were to attract entries from a wide range of marques including Ferrari, Maserati, Veritas, AFM, HWM, Cisitalia, Gordini, Connaught and Cooper, they could stage attractive races cheaply. In all, 31 races for Formula 2 cars were organised in Europe in 1950. Of these the Scuderia Ferrari contrived to have entries in 15, sometimes, as at Roubaix, by entering the Ferrari of a private owner.

Alberto Ascari was entered by Ferrari in nine of these races, six of which he won, driving a new de Dion-axled 12-cylinder F2 Ferrari. He scored his wins at Modena, Mons, Rome, Reims, the Nürburgring and Lake Garda. At Mettet he won his heat but had a rear axle fail in the final. In the other two races he finished second behind team-mate Gigi Villoresi. By any standards this was an excellent record.

Also on Alberto's schedule in 1950 were a few sports-car races. Engine lubrication let him down in the Giro di Sicilia and in the Mille Miglia a rear-axle bearing seized before he reached Rome. In August he and Serafini drove from Italy to England by way of the Nürburgring in the two Type 166 Barchettas they would race in the *Daily Express* meeting. There they were comfortable one–two winners.

In the bar of the cross-Channel ferry heading for Dover the two Italians had met Rodney Walkerley and photographer Louis Klemantaski, returning from the German GP. Unsure of the route from Dover to London and wary of driving on the left, they suggested that the two Britons drive the Ferraris on the last leg! 'Klem' found himself accompanied by Ascari and revelled in the Barchetta's wonderful performance. 'I gradually became aware that, much to my dismay, Alberto was getting slightly agitated,' he wrote. 'Speech was not possible so I made gestures of inquiry. He then pointed to the gear lever and held up five fingers to indicate that there was still a fifth gear to use! I found the higher gear and changed up while Alberto snuggled down and went to sleep.'

Ferrari had a new strategy for the 1950 Formula 1 season as well. With the help of Aurelio Lampredi he had begun planning for it in 1949. Implementation would begin in 1950. Key to that implementation were the skills of Alberto Ascari, now 31. No longer were journalists obliged to mention that he was the son of a famous father. The son was making history of his own.

Ascari warmly congratulates Ferrari team-mate Gigi Villoresi on his victory in the Dutch Grand Prix on 31 July 1949. Alberto is lucky to survive the loss of a front wheel only six laps from the finish of the second heat.

Siam's Prince Bira in a 4CLT/48 Maserati is Ascari's closest challenger at the start of the 1949 Swiss Grand Prix. Nevertheless Alberto, running a light fuel load, slashes into the early lead that is to become his trademark.

After engine difficulties in practice (opposite top) the Ferraris are not greatly favoured for the Swiss race. Ascari is about to lap the 4CL Maserati of Antonio Branca (opposite bottom) on his way to a great victory for Ferrari.

Ascari leaps into the lead of the final of the Daily Express *International Trophy race on 20 August 1949. Challenging him in the San Remo Maseratis just behind are, left to right,* Prince Bira, Reg Parnell, and Nino Farina. Alberto wins the approval of Ferrari's team manager by fighting off a strong challenge from a determined Farina.

Alberto Ascari comes to think well of Britain and the British after his August 1949 Silverstone visit, to which he and Dorino Serafini drive in their 2-litre Ferrari Barchettas. He and Serafini finish first and second respectively in the production sports-car race, Ascari using both his cloth cap and a visored helmet during the warm weekend. Ascari and Serafini flank the trophy with team manager Federico Giberti at the left next to mechanic Pasquale Cassani.

Although intensely critical of his own performances, Alberto Ascari is entirely satisfied with a superb victory in the new GP49 Ferrari in the Grand Prix of Europe at Monza on 11 September 1949. His Monza test two weeks before the race (opposite) leads to Ferrari's decision to enter the new car designed by Colombo (above left in white shirt). Although suffering from a toothache, Ascari is well able to take pleasure in a fine race.

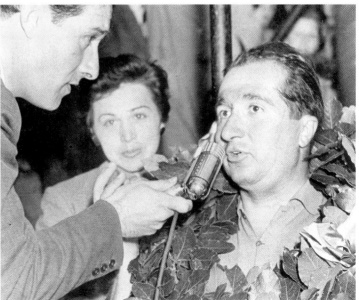

When the Ferrari works sends a team to Argentina during the winter of 1949–50 Alberto Ascari scores two victories in the supercharged 2-litre car sponsored by an aperitif maker. He is chasing Fangio's similar car on the seashore at Mar del Plata (above) and spinning ignominiously at the start of the Evita Perón Trophy race at Palermo Park (above right). Racing away are, left to right, Serafini, Villoresi and Fangio.

In 1950 Ferrari enters his new ace in many Formula 2 contests. On 7 May at Modena (above) Ascari collects the hardware for fastest qualifier, fastest lap and race victory.

Three weeks later at Monza (below and opposite bottom) he falls to second in the final after a long pit stop to check the front suspension but still deserves a kiss and a bouquet.

The first post-war German Grand Prix is held for Formula 2 cars on 20 August 1950. Ascari is the wire to wire winner. At the start (preceding pages) Ascari is flanked by the Gordini of eventual second-place man André Simon (88) and Serafini's Ferrari (4). Veritas-mounted are Karl Kling (64) and Toni Ulmen (44). Before the race Ascari chats (above left) with fellow motorcycle racer Ernst Henne, on the right, and drives down the pit lane chased by the unmistakable figure of Alfred Neubauer (above).

At the Turin Salon in May 1950 Ferrari shows off his three team drivers, Serafini and Ascari flanking Villoresi (above). Ascari meets there with Milan Ferrari dealer Franco Cornacchia, who organises the Ferrari Mexican Road Race entries in 1951 and 1952 (above right). The team-mates share a Toblerone at Berne in 1949 and are joined at Monza in 1950 by Corrado Filippini, left, and journalist Ernst Hornickel.

At Garda in October 1950 Ascari cheerfully signs an autograph (left) and contemplates his prospects (above) with Franco Cortese, left, and team manager Giberti, who is seen on the pit counter at Monza in May 1950 (below) with Filippini and Ascari. At Silverstone in 1949 the winner receives the congratulations of Stirling Moss (below left).

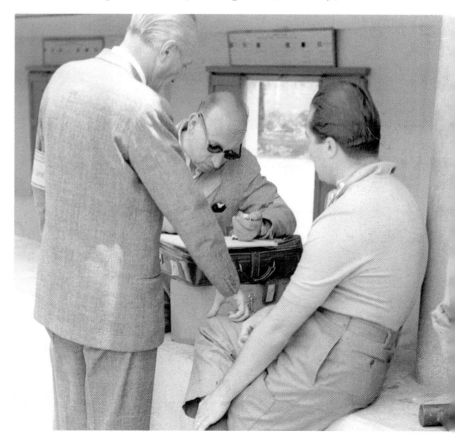

The atmosphere of Formula 2 racing on the roads of Italy is captured by Rodolfo Mailander at Garda on 15 October 1950. Alongside Alberto at the start are the Gordini (6) of Branca and the Ferrari of Stagnoli (2). In the streets of the town he laps an Osca en route to his sixth and final Formula 2 victory of the season.

CHAPTER 4

Alfa breaker

The new GP49 Formula 1 Ferrari had barely been ready for Alberto Ascari to drive it to victory in the European Grand Prix at Monza in September 1949. The GP49 was an ambitious design by Gioachino Colombo; indeed it seemed that only an ambitious design would be capable of defeating the Alfa Romeo 'Alfetta' – which was also the work of Colombo. With its 12 cylinders, four cams and two superchargers the Ferrari bristled with exotica. Yet hidden in the water passages of its cylinder heads were design faults that meant that it would never reliably produce the power of which it was theoretically capable. Ascari's feat in winning with it at Monza was indeed a worthy tribute to his father.

Flawed or not, this costly creation was Ferrari's principal weapon for the opening of the 1950 racing season, in which six selected national GP races would award points to their top five finishers that would count toward a world drivers' championship. (The 'world' part was bolstered by the inclusion of the Indianapolis 500-mile

Driving the difficult GP49 Ferrari, Ascari finishes second in the 1950 Monaco Grand Prix on 21 May. Afterward he will find a charming way to complain to Enzo Ferrari about the car's rough gearbox.

race among the qualifying events, although it was run to a different set of rules.) Drivers could count their four best results and a fastest race lap was good for a bonus point. With Alfa's return it was expected to be a competitive season. Maserati was entering works cars and expectations were great for the first appearance of Britain's powerful supercharged V16 BRM.

The initial Alfa-Ferrari contest was inconclusive. Wet weather spoiled the San Remo meeting on 16 April that saw Ascari and Villoresi in two of the new cars against a lone Alfa driven by Fangio. From his pole position Ascari led from the start but – perhaps keeping too close an eye on his temperature gauge – spun and let the Argentine by. Chasing hard to catch him, Alberto was closing the gap when he left the road again, this time hitting the adjacent landscape and retiring.

'I don't know much about Ascari's accident at San Remo,' Fangio said later. 'The fact is that I had already passed him and was in the lead at the time of his crash. What I do remember is that there was an article in some paper that said that I was a good driver but that I was up against the barriers all the time. In fact it was Ascari that was up against the barriers.' The Italian media had not been too welcoming to foreigner Fangio, awarded as he was a coveted seat in a Type 158 Alfa.

Ferrari failed to nominate a team for the first championship qualifying event at Silverstone but sent three cars to the next at Monte Carlo in May for Ascari, Villoresi and Sommer. There the field was drastically depleted by a first-lap crash that eliminated nine cars, including all the Alfas but Fangio's. Ascari slipped into second place but Villoresi was severely delayed. He drove through the remaining field to pass Alberto into second before retiring with axle trouble. Needing two fuel stops to Fangio's one, Ascari finished second more than a lap in arrears.

The post-Monte Carlo debriefing showed an Ascari attribute that was of great value to his relationship with Ferrari, Romolo Tavoni recalled. 'Alberto was a pleasant, agreeable person,' he said, who 'had friendly relations with everyone. He had a particular ability to tell Enzo Ferrari things that Ferrari wouldn't tolerate from anyone else. For instance: back from the Monaco GP he said to the Old Man, "Well, your gearbox is reliable, very strong indeed. But look at my hands, please, and see the state they are in. After the race, back in the paddock, there were some very nice girls eager to get my autograph … but I had to refuse. I simply couldn't sign!" Ferrari laughed, but took note of it and at once ordered his technicians to improve the operation of the gearbox.'

In qualifying for the next points race at Berne the two Ferraris were some four seconds a lap slower than the Alfas and only five seconds faster than the best unblown Talbot-Lagos – not a promising prospect. Alberto kept his car among the Alfas for the first two laps of the Swiss GP but then fell back and retired with a failed oil scavenge pump.

The Belgian Grand Prix of 1949 had shown the potential of the unsupercharged 4½-litre GP car when Louis Rosier went through non-stop in his Talbot-Lago to defeat the 1½-litre supercharged Ferraris. Now, at the same race a year later, Ferrari presented a car that showed that it was capable of learning new lessons about GP technology. Its chassis was that of the supercharged models but under its bonnet was an unblown V12 of 3.3 litres. The new car was assigned to Ascari.

This was the first fruit of a project that began in 1949 when Aurelio Lampredi argued that the best way to beat the Alfas was with an unblown 4½-litre car. The same advice was given Ferrari by Raymond Sommer, who had driven both the unsupercharged 4½-litre Talbots and the GP Ferraris and, before the war, the 158 Alfas as well. To finance this all-new engine Enzo Ferrari turned to Pirelli, his tyre supplier, requesting and receiving a grant of some $20,000 for this purpose, £8,000. The amount seemed so small to Piero Pirelli that he double-checked to make sure that that was all Ferrari really needed.

Although 4.5 litres was the eventual target, the engine was first raced at 3.3 litres for two reasons. One was that Ferrari liked to develop big engines from smaller ones. The other was that the existing drive line was only able to cope with the torque of the new V12 in 3.3-litre form. Ascari was already familiar with the engine; in a lower state of tune it powered the 275S sports Barchetta he had driven in the Mille Miglia.

Qualifying for the Spa race, Ascari was two seconds (out of some 280) slower than Villoresi's four-cam supercharged Ferrari and a dozen seconds off the Alfa pace. Making one planned fuel stop in the 307-mile race, Alberto suffered other stops to replace failed tyres. He placed fifth a lap behind the leaders and a lap ahead of Villoresi. It was a low-key performance that nevertheless carried the seeds of future promise. The next step was to develop a new chassis to take the engine.

The fast French GP at Reims received entries from Ferrari but the team, busy with its new project, failed to appear. The non-championship Formula 1 race at Bari in July was one in which Ferrari liked to try out new cars, and it intended to do so in 1950. When tests showed the car to be unready, however, it sent Alberto and Gigi to do battle in Formula 2 models. This was a wasted journey with both cars failing, Villoresi's after it had been taken over by Ascari – an odd manoeuvre in a race not counting for championship points.

Neither were points on offer for the next few Formula 1 races through July and August. The same supercharged cars as at Spa went to Albi for a two-heat race for which, embarrassingly, they qualified six to ten seconds slower than 4CLT/48 Maseratis. Mercifully both retired, Ascari's in the second heat. For the Dutch GP at Zandvoort Alberto was given an F2 car, as at Bari. He gave it a determined drive to third place.

In those days Geneva, Switzerland, enjoyed a Grand Prix on its streets, the GP des Nations – an apt title for a race in this city of many international organisations. The third such race saw an excellent entry of current F1 cars and also, at last, the pukka unsupercharged 1950 Ferrari with its de Dion rear suspension and uprated brakes. While Villoresi's had the 3.3-litre engine Ascari's was powered by a 4.1-litre V12. They were challenged by no less than four Alfettas.

His new car restored Alberto Ascari to the front row of the grid, two seconds slower than pole-sitter Fangio's Alfa. Villoresi equalled his time so the two Ferraris were ahead of the other three Alfas at the start. In the race Alberto kept his second place behind Fangio right through to six laps before the finish, when a valve dropped and destroyed a piston and cylinder. He was still classified fourth. Gigi was running fifth until he skidded after hitting oil and veered through barriers, not only injuring himself severely but also killing three spectators and injuring 20 others. Tragic though this was, Ascari could not resist pointing out that Villoresi had been so rash as to pick up and pet a black kitten before the race.

At the end of August Ascari was deputed by Enzo Ferrari to pack his bag for England and Silverstone. He had sold one of his four-cam supercharged Formula 1 cars to British bearing maker Tony Vandervell, who shrewdly arranged for Ascari to pilot it in the International Trophy race. During Ascari's visit Vandervell showed him around the Norton works, of which he was a director, and offered him a run on a Norton motorcycle. The racing was a disappointment, with Alberto befuddled by oil fumes in his heat and spinning off. As the previous chapter relates he had a better run in the supporting sports-car race.

In September the teams were again at Monza for the Italian Grand Prix, which this time enjoyed an entry of four Alfa Romeos. Against them were two of the new Ferraris, now with full 4.5-litre engines. 'Milan was in something of a ferment when I arrived on the Wednesday before race day,' wrote Rodney Walkerley, 'for Alberto Ascari had just done an unofficial practice lap at Monza in 1min 59secs.' Not since Sanesi lapped in 2:0.4 in 1948 had anyone gone faster at Monza. In official practice Alberto reduced his time to 1:58.8, which only Fangio managed to undercut at the end of the session and then by a scant fifth of a second.

Ranked in rows of four, the field stormed away from the grid with Ascari lagging at first, but, recorded Walkerley, 'two miles later he slashed past [Fangio] into second place and sat on Farina's tail, two lengths away, at 150mph. Decent.' For a pair of laps he even led Farina to test his intentions and then slipped back to second, knowing that the Alfas would have to stop for fuel while he would not. But at 21 of the 80 laps the big Ferrari's axle gave out and Alberto walked back to the pits from his abandoned car.

Meanwhile Dorino Serafini was running third in the sister 375F1. At lap 48, wrote Walkerley, 'Serafini stopped for wheels, whereupon the crowd went mad and hit each other on the head with Chianti bottles, for Ascari took over and roared off back into the battle.' When Luigi Fagioli's Alfa stopped for fuel Alberto moved into second, where he remained to the finish behind the winner, Alfa-mounted Nino Farina. The victory confirmed him as the first-ever World Champion. Ascari ranked fifth with 11 points against Farina's 30.

Wrapping up the Formula 1 season was a non-championship 194-mile race at Barcelona that drew a strong entry apart from Alfa Romeo, absent after clinching Farina's award. The vaunted British BRMs made a rare appearance, one of them joining the three Ferraris in the front row of the grid. Both retired, however, and the race was led from start to finish by Alberto Ascari in the latest Ferrari. He set the fastest lap for good measure. In this two-thirds-length GP no Ferrari had to stop for either fuel or tyres. It was a good omen for 1951.

'Apart from Sommer,' wrote Rodney Walkerley at the season's end, 'the outstanding drivers of the year were the quiet, reserved Argentine Juan Manuel Fangio, whose courtesy on the circuit was matched only by his immense verve, and the genial Alberto Ascari, a comparative newcomer who now ranks with Fangio in speed, determination and polished skill.' For 1951 Ferrari would furnish him with a mount worthy of his burgeoning talent.

Looking ahead to the new season, Ascari told Nino Nutrizio that 'the most important race is the one I'm about to take part in. The main thing I worry about throughout the race is being prepared to face the unexpected, so as to overcome it in the best possible way. I know the track, I know my possibilities and that of the car. The secret of a real driver is being able to drive to the limit. By limit I mean the maximum speed at which you can go without running off the road.' Only once in 1951 did he knowingly exceed that limit and he did so, perhaps, because of the impossibility of 'knowing the track'.

The track in this case was the Mille Miglia, which seemed determined to be unkind to Ascari. Here was a race which had first been run in 1927, so Alberto was free to make his own mark. His father could not have participated. Yet it was slow to yield to his skills. Not long after the start in 1951 Ascari, startled by headlight beams from a side road, left the highway at a point where, sadly, some spectators were standing. Among those injured by his 3-litre Ferrari was a prominent local doctor, who later succumbed.

As is obligatory in Italy, manslaughter charges were brought against Ascari for the physician's death. It took three years for the case to be settled and for the driver to be cleared of personal responsibility. In the meantime Ascari resolved not to race in the Mille Miglia. His focus would be on the Formula races in which he excelled.

No black-cat stories were associated with the Mille Miglia crash but the felines were out in force at Marseilles for a Formula 2 race in April. When he left his hotel for practice 'a black cat slid between my legs. I tempted fate all the same and went out onto the track. After four laps the brakes seized suddenly and I was thrown out of the car.' On the next morning 'this devil cat, bounding in front of me, took refuge under my car. During the race, while I was passing a slower Frenchman, he suddenly and without reason went outwards. To avoid hitting him I had to veer off, my car slamming against the hard hay bales, irreparably damaging my steering.' He had been leading at the time.

Luckily Alberto was uninjured in these crashes. He was less fortunate in a F2 race at Genoa in May in an incident that could have been much more serious. He was leading when his fuel tank sprang a leak. He stopped for a top-up but a few laps later the car caught alight. Ascari calmly stopped and was climbing out when a foot snagged in the steering wheel. Driver Biondetti was among those who helped him from the now-brightly-burning Ferrari. Alberto suffered second-degree burns to his right forearm but was otherwise unharmed.

Concentrating now on Formula 1, Enzo Ferrari was less committed to Formula 2 in 1951. In fact he sold most of his stable of 2-litre racers to the Marzotto brothers – better known for their Mille Miglia successes – who continued to fly the flag for Ferrari. Ascari was entered by the works in five F2 events in '51. Marseilles and Genoa have already been mentioned. In the other three, Monza, Naples, and Modena, he was victorious, indeed overwhelmingly so.

At Naples Ascari had taken appropriate precautions, Gigi Villoresi recalled: 'I went to collect him from the station at five o'clock in the morning. To get to our hotel in the city centre, there was a long, wide avenue. Alberto was driving when suddenly he slammed on the brakes! A black cat was crossing that avenue. We now made a detour such as I have never known, through obscure side streets and back alleys just to arrive at our hotel from a different route. When we did arrive I had fallen asleep!'

Happily Villoresi was now recovered from his Geneva injuries. In fact he had been present at Barcelona the previous October – though still using a cane – to support the Ferrari team there. Not involved this year in the Argentine races, the inseparable pair opened their 1951 account instead in February in the snow of the Sestrière ski resort in the Alps near Turin. Driving a Lancia Aurelia saloon they won the Sestrière Rally.

Their first proper Formula 1 race was in mid-March on a new road circuit on the outskirts of the historic Sicilian city of Syracuse. Nothing there could threaten their 4½-litre V12s, which took turns leading until Alberto drew away, only to be stopped by engine trouble. At Pau later in the month the story was the same, except that gearbox failure stopped Alberto's Ferrari. In both cases Villoresi collected the win.

Ascari's first racing victory of the year came in April at San Remo, where he had a new 375F1 with dual ignition. The first race for the championship was in May at Berne for the Swiss Grand Prix. After his burns the week before at Genoa Alberto was not on top form, but even so it was obvious that Alfa Romeo had not been idle over the winter. Fangio and Farina were dominant at first but a newcomer to the Ferrari team, Piero Taruffi, took the fight to them and finished second behind Fangio in a wet race. Ascari was sixth, just out of the points.

Two weeks later in mid-June the teams met again at the fast and unforgiving Spa circuit for the Belgian GP.

Here the Alfas had an advantage in practice but when their tanks were full for the race the Ferraris were much closer. Villoresi was out early and Alberto made a stop on the 15th lap of 36 for fuel and rear tyres. From then on he settled into second behind winner Farina. The need to change tyres, forced by the high speeds these cars were reaching, kept Ferrari from fully exploiting its fuel-consumption advantage over the thirsty Alfas.

Battle was rejoined under the hot sun of the Champagne region at Reims in July. 'The scene at the start was Grand Prix racing at its most typical and there-fore most French,' reported Rodney Walkerley. 'The cars were wheeled forth one by one, drivers walking along-side while a gendarmerie guard of honour presented carbines and the National Anthems were duly played – all very like the Entry of the Gladiators.'

At Reims Ascari joined two Alfas on the front row of the grid and commanded the lead in the early laps. Soon, however, 'registering emotion,' wrote Walkerley, he pitted 'to mention he had few brakes and not enough gears' before retiring. As team leader, Ascari was entitled to take over the car of another Ferrari driver, with whom he would share any points that they jointly earned. A newcomer to the team, Argentine Froilán González, was lying second when he stopped for tyres and fuel at mid-race and Alberto leaped into his racer's seat. He moved the Ferrari into the lead for a few laps but had to stop for a brake adjustment. This pit stop was more or less his one-minute deficit at the finish of a hard-fought race, second behind Fangio.

Their rivalry was intensifying that summer as a lady friend, Mila Schön, observed: 'They were really rivals. Not enemies, I mean. Just rivals. On the tracks, obvi-ously, but outside as well, even if with a touch of irony. After the race at Reims we were invited to a party organ-ised by champagne producers. In a huge hall they had built platforms from champagne cases. One was for Alfa Romeo, another for Ferrari, a third for Maserati and so on. People were invited to dance on the platforms. Fangio came to our table and invited me to dance. I would have accepted but Alberto promptly got up, took me by the hand and, looking at Fangio and laughing, said: "Never with him!" Okay, he was kidding – but I'm not sure he was *completely* kidding.'

The rivals next assembled at Silverstone for the British

GP, a sobersided event without all that French folderol. There in practice all the runners were put in the shade by the speed of González, who found the fast, flat turns of the former airfield just to his liking. The slower Ascari, said mechanic Ener Vecchi, was 'protesting because he found the brakes didn't work as he wanted. We had a team meeting to find out and hopefully to fix what wasn't okay. Ascari was getting a bit nervy but González put a hand on his shoulder and with his funny accent said, "But press your foot, *muchacho*, the brakes are there, for sure!" Everybody laughed, Ascari included, and the tension subsided.

'The following day González was an unrestrained fury,' Vecchi added. 'Ascari was well behind and after half the race had to retire with a broken gearbox. Soon afterward González came into the pits for fuel and generously offered his car to Alberto, who refused, urging him to start again at once toward his well-deserved victory.' With a slight smile Alberto placed his hand on the Argentine's shoulder as he sought to dismount. It was, said Vecchi, 'a good deed. But in those days gestures like that weren't so rare.' González roared on to an historic victory over the Alfa Romeos.

The victory was a watershed, not only for Grand Prix racing but within the Ferrari team, said Aurelio Lampredi: 'My friend and "brother" Alberto Ascari arrived willingly at Maranello, but from the outset it seemed as if, at the back of his mind, there lingered doubts about our Ferrari car: "Yes, it is a beautiful car, however the Alfa …" But when Pepe González scored that first true victory in the 4.5 at Silverstone, for Alberto the myth of Alfa was at once dispelled and he was 110 per cent with us.'

Ascari's fresh commitment and confidence were powerfully in evidence at the German Grand Prix at the Nürburgring at the end of July. On this 14¼-mile circuit with its 174 corners, the world's most demanding, Ascari set the fastest practice lap at an average of 85.7mph to become one of only three drivers to break the ten-minute barrier. Although Fangio held an early lead in the race, Ascari soon assumed and retained command.

Late in the race Alberto made a surprise pit stop for fresh rear tyres. 'His pit staff seemed somewhat amazed to see him and there was a certain amount of drama before the jack was under the car,' wrote Walkerley.

Insight into this was offered by Giovanni Canestrini, who during a pre-race post-prandial walk was asked by the driver, 'How did Nuvolari win against the Germans in 1935?' Canestrini 'recounted Tazio's great undertaking, when he beat Von Brauchitsch, who had to abandon the race on the last lap owing to a flat tyre a few kilometres from the finish.

'It only came to me the next day that Ascari's question was premeditated,' Canestrini added. 'He told me so himself after the race. Knowing well Fangio's tactic of attacking his rivals at the end of the race – generally the most critical and delicate phase – he did not want to run the risk of wearing out his tyres, as had happened to Brauchitsch on the last laps, when he would have to react to the pace imposed by his pursuer: "Being certain that I could go as fast as Fangio, I wanted to be in the best condition to beat him."'

Ascari could have let his pit staff in on his plan, but he didn't. Had he done so, he may well have feared that it could leak to Fangio through his friend González, who was still on the Ferrari strength. Instead the last stop was indeed a surprise and one with an extra dimension of satisfaction for the driver, as Alberto explained: 'I came in because otherwise people would have said that I won because I made only one pit stop. Instead I also made two stops – and one of them a *surprise*!' This was consistent with a character trait that Piero Casucci explained: 'He wanted to be in tune with his conscience. A success which was not satisfactory above all was not a success to be taken into consideration.' The 'Ring success fully met his criterion. Jubilant in the winner's circle, he reached out to kiss the two mechanics who changed his tyres.

Two non-championship F1 races followed. In the first at Pescara Ascari was knocked out only a kilometre from the start by oil-pressure problems that had also loomed during practice. At Bari he was chasing Fangio's Alfa, setting the fastest race lap, when a mechanical failure threw the Ferrari into a sudden spin and retired it. Watching the drivers in practice and the race was Stirling Moss:

'Alberto Ascari was rather better than just good, he was very good indeed. He may have been as fast as Fangio, but he had not got the polish that so distinguished Fangio. I remember watching both of them in a certain corner in the Bari Grand Prix. Fangio would come around and just brush along the straw bales, not touching them, just alongside them, beautiful. Ascari, when he came through, would just clip the kerb and straighten out, just a slight oversteer with power but every time he was just clipping the kerb. Fangio was on the identical line but he wasn't touching anything. I think that was about the extent of the difference, and it's a big difference.'

Another close observer, Villoresi, begged to differ: 'In those days Fangio was certainly not superior to Alberto. Alberto's style was one of force and vehemence, very clean, where he took up a position on a curve. Fangio, often extremely lucky, initiated the style of side-slipping.' Ascari's style was the dominant one in the next points race at Monza. The Alfas could not match his winning pace. Thereafter Alberto could count on 25 points and Juan Manuel on 27. The final 275 racing miles in Spain would decide the world-champion driver.

Ferrari denied Ascari the championship. The driver did all that could have been expected, putting his car on pole and leading the Barcelona race. But almost at once the team Ferraris started shedding tyre treads. This was blamed at the time on their use of 16-inch wheels instead of the more usual 17-inch or even the 18-inch wheels favoured by Alfa Romeo. Ruefully, however, Lampredi later blamed the failures on the way in which the tyres had been inflated. Ascari had to stop three times in all for fresh tyres, which dropped him to fourth at the finish. Fangio, the winner, was champion.

This was an expensive result for Fangio. Before the race the two rivals had struck an agreement: 'Whoever wins the title pays the bill. The loser chooses the restaurant and invites the guests.' On the Thursday following the race almost 50 guests gathered at Milan's Savini restaurant in the Galleria del Duomo for what was described as a 'marvellous party'.

Over the winter Alberto Ascari was chosen as Italy's Athlete of 1951. A charming photo shows him holding the medal, which is tiny. Although brief, its caption speaks volumes: 'The medal is small, but Ascari is big.'

In the snows of Sestrière, partnered by Villoresi, Ascari pilots a Lancia Aurelia to victory in the rally held on 23–26 February 1951. It is a bracing change from his usual winter in the heat of Argentina.

Fangio leads from the start of the 1950 Monaco GP with Ascari in mid-field at far right. Alberto is delayed by the first-lap crash that eliminates almost half the field but recovers to soldier on to second in spite of an erratic engine and burns to his left foot. Fresh goggles are proffered at a pit stop, which Charles Faroux observes from the right.

1950 is a year of transition in Formula 1 for Ferrari and for Ascari, who drives the ambitious but flawed GP49 at Monaco on 21 May (below) and two weeks later at Berne (above), where he retires early. On 31 July in the non-championship Geneva GP he drives the new unblown Ferrari in 4.1-litre form (opposite), here leading the Maserati of Franco Rol. He copes with all the Alfas save Fangio's before retiring. He is well up at the start at Geneva (overleaf top) and storms off the line at San Remo on 22 April 1951 (overleaf bottom) to the right of Villoresi and the Maserati of de Graffenried.

Scenes at Monza in September 1950 portray the close attention that Enzo Ferrari gives to the son of the man who was once his role model in the racing world. At Monza Ascari is second, seriously challenging the Alfa hegemony for the first time. With the Ferrari's latest version he wins at San Remo on 22 April 1951 (opposite).

Although he practises in a cloth cap, Ascari dons a motorcycle-type helmet for the GP race at Reims on 1 July 1951. He leads the Alfas in the early laps (above), but retires and takes over the car of González, with which he chases team-mate Villoresi (opposite) to take second place in the Champagne country.

Clockwise from top left: Ascari checks the controls of the Ferrari he drives in the 1950 Swiss Grand Prix, settles into his Formula 2 Ferrari at Pau in the same year, signs autographs as the winner of

the German Grand Prix in 1951, and tries the cockpit of the BRM at Silverstone in 1951. Regular driver Peter Walker is helmeted as Ascari discusses the V16 with BRM's Raymond Mays.

Fangio and Ascari are addressed by Corrado Filippini at Monte Carlo in 1950 (above left) and prepare for the start at Monza the same year (below right). At Monza in 1951 Alberto

is joined by journalist Canestrini (bottom left). Ascari and Villoresi sort the contents of their precious racing kits at Barcelona in October 1951 (above right).

Rudy Mailander is in the Ferrari pit at the 1951 German Grand Prix when Ascari makes a surprise visit for fresh rear tyres and a squirt of fuel three laps before the finish. At the 'Ring (preceding pages) he administers a sound thrashing to the Alfas. He is seen bareheaded in the flying Ferrari.

Before the start of a rainy GP race at Berne on 27 May 1951 (top, both pages, from left) Fangio expostulates to Ascari with González and Lampredi standing by. Alberto expresses his view in return. Joined by Alfa driver Consalvo Sanesi, Ascari shrugs with white-helmeted Villoresi behind him. Team-mate González gives Alberto a reassuring embrace.

In 1951's Formula 2 racing (opposite bottom) Ascari leads from the start at Marseilles ahead of Gordinis and HWMs. He stays in front through 70 of the 90 laps until he retires with faulty steering after being edged into the hay bales by another competitor. His 1951 Mille Miglia ends not far from the start at Brescia (below) in a crash.

Although the Alfa Romeos of Fangio and Farina lead some of the early laps in the Italian Grand Prix at Monza on 16 September 1951 (opposite), Ascari (2) takes command for good on the 14th of the race's 80 laps. He follows Fangio (above) through the Vialone bend, a curve that will be fateful for Ascari in 1955. His win at Monza (right) brings him close to Fangio in the championship but the Argentine prevails in the season's final race at Barcelona. Ascari is named Italy's Athlete of the Year (overleaf), for which 'The medal is small, but Ascari is big'.

With its short wheelbase and rear swing axles the super-charged Formula 1 Ferrari of 1949 was anything but bid-dable, but Ascari drove it to second in his heat and victory in the final of the International Trophy at Silverstone on 20 August (above and preceding page).

Stability was better with the longer wheelbase and de Dion suspension of the 4½-litre GP Ferrari that Ascari drove to fourth in Spain at the end of the 1951 season (below). In 1952 he made a dramatic appearance at Indianapolis with a similar car (opposite and overleaf top).

With good reason, Alberto Ascari became indelibly associated with the marvellous Ferrari Type 500 'Starlet' that he raced to his two World Championships in 1952 and 1953. He was second behind Fangio at the start of the 1953 German Grand Prix (bottom of preceding spread, above, and overleaf) but soon went into the lead, of which he was only deprived by a missing front wheel. In July 1952 Ascari was the winner of the British Grand Prix at Silverstone (opposite).

Alberto Ascari remained true to his blue racing kit, be it in the helmeted era of the 1950s at the Nürburgring (opposite) or when cloth helmets were worn during the late 1940s at Silverstone (top left). Ascari is seen in his raincoat at Silverstone (top right) and having a mock tussle with Karl Kling before the start of the French GP at Reims in 1954 (below). His utter intensity is evident as he prepares to compete at Monaco in 1955 (right).

Ascari is on the front row next to the silver Mercedes of Fangio and Kling for the start of the 1954 French GP (above), but his borrowed Maserati 250F doesn't last long. His new Lancia D50 becomes raceworthy only at the end of 1954.

On 16 January 1955 he races the Lancia in Argentina, starting from the front row (opposite) and leading for many of the early laps before spinning off and crashing. The Lancia is still visibly quite a handful.

With two victories in minor F1 races behind them, Ascari and the Lancia team are ready to attack the 1955 Grand Prix of Monaco (above). Alberto checks the mirrors of his D50, chas-sis number 0006 (opposite). In qualifying (overleaf) he and Fangio have equal fastest times. The race, in which he crashes into the harbour, is fated to be his last.

CHAPTER 5

Clean sweep

Ascari was a keen and capable skier. Nevertheless after two warm winters in South America his 1950–51 sojourn in the snows of Sestrière left him yearning for a bit of sun. Relief for him and Villoresi came when Ferrari decided to accept an invitation from the Mexican government to send two cars to compete in the Carrera Panamericana, a race to celebrate the completion of the Mexican portion of a highway linking the Americas. The second 'Mexican Road Race' was held from 20 to 25 November 1951, the cars racing 1,934 miles in eight legs from the south of Mexico to the north.

How did two Ferraris qualify to compete in a race for production saloon cars? They didn't, really, but Vignale – then doing a lot of work for Ferrari – made quite a good job of bodying two 212 Inter chassis with shapes that passed muster as four-seater cars. They were prepared

After his victory at Monza in the final qualifying race of his first World Championship year of 1952, Alberto Ascari is deservedly in the limelight. In August at Comminges, in the penultimate race of the parallel French Formula 2 championship, he takes the chequered flag from Charles Faroux (preceding page). After his own Ferrari's steering fails he takes over the sister car of André Simon to win with a margin of more than a lap from team-mate Nino Farina.

by Scuderia Guastalla, run from Milan by Ferrari dealer Franco Cornacchia, and sponsored by Sinclair oil. One was to be driven by the Ascari/Villoresi pairing and the other by Piero Taruffi with Luigi Chinetti, who was also responsible for maintaining the cars. Guastalla provided no mechanics. The drivers did all their own servicing under Chinetti's direction.

A rival team's engineer said that at the start of the race 'Villoresi seemed very unhappy and talked rapidly to his co-pilot, Alberto Ascari, second ranking driver of the world.' This could have concerned their disagreement over the exhaust system. 'Alberto wanted to get rid of the steel wool from the silencer and free the exhaust pipe,' Villoresi recalled. 'He was sure that not only would the car make more noise but it would also go much faster. I thought exactly the opposite. I knew from experience that one drives faster in a quiet car, for the simple reason that noise increases the impression of speed. Without the wool our Ferrari would only have made more noise.'

The noise the Ferraris made was impressive enough. An observer recalled them 'winding out in a banshee scream with the gear shifts coming so rapidly as to be indistinguishable.' The twisty, mountainous first leg from

Tuxtla Gutiérrez to Oaxaca was expected to be a dream for the nimble Ferraris, competing against American saloons weighing twice as much. It became a nightmare instead, with the Pirelli tyres shedding tread after tread. 'If Ferrari had seen us on the first leg he would have put us on the Grand Prix tyre-changing team,' Ascari joked. 'We were fast and good. First one then another, six times we jacked up the car and changed tyres during the first leg. And each time the operation went faster. Unfortunately, however, this forced the car to slow, and we reached Oaxaca at a few dozen miles per hour.' They finished the leg 45th among 91 starters but fortunately within the maximum time that allowed them to continue in the race.

'Gigi was driving on that now-famous first leg,' Ascari continued. 'He was really good and managed to salvage the salvageable.' Running next on Mexican Goodyears, matters improved. Ascari: 'The second leg, and first victory, was mine. Then we alternated for the rest of the race, a stretch for one and then a stretch for the other. The Americans and Mexicans didn't expect such performance from the Ferraris. They were all convinced the Italian cars would be better on the mixed portions, but no-one believed our cars could also dominate on the endless, fast straights. When the straights began, we astonished competitors and spectators. Gigi and I both got a kick out of it as one by one we gobbled up the other cars. A real good time at over 120mph.'

'The engines ran perfectly without as much as a sneeze,' recalled Gigi Villoresi. 'In adjusting the carburation Ascari was great. He became the expert on jets, air horns and choke tubes' to adjust the engines to cope with the huge altitude variations from one end of Mexico to the other. The Ferraris quickly recovered from their poor early form to seize the race leadership, with the Taruffi/Chinetti team in the van thanks to fewer tyre problems on the first leg. They were in the lead by the end of the third leg, and after the fourth stage 'Ciccio' and Gigi were second behind them after winning several stages. Running to team orders they finished the race eight minutes in arrears at an average speed of 87.53mph.

'Alberto and I had complete faith in each other's driving skills,' Villoresi recalled after this demanding event. 'We both accepted constructive criticism from the other, and there was never a cross word. This was the result of a long friendship and mutual respect. Every now and again we played jokes on each other. I remember a buffet in a big hotel in Mexico City. Out of curiosity I tasted a kind of Mexican chilli. It was so hot I thought I would die. I turned toward Alberto, who liked his food, and pointed to the deadly chillies. He bit into one boldly. He nearly killed me.

'We left for Milan the day after the prizegiving,' Gigi continued. 'There was never any time and we had to live economically, especially during the years with Ferrari.' Between the overall prizes and those for stage victories the Guastalla team grossed $37,667 for placing first and second but not much was left after subtracting the substantial expenses of shipping two cars to Mexico. They didn't have to be shipped back; they were sold to eager Mexicans.

Just before the racers left for Mexico the news had broken of the future plans for Formula 1. The new Formula taking effect in 1954 would be for cars with 2½-litre unsupercharged engines and 750cc supercharged engines. There would be no subsidiary 'Formula 2' Meanwhile, the current 1½-litre blown/4½-litre unblown Formula 1 was falling into disuse. Alfa Romeo, having won everything there was to win, declined to continue. Ferrari would compete; it prepared a new version of its successful 375F1. But after the frequent and celebrated non-appearances of the V16 BRM, in the spring of 1952 race organisers despaired of having decent fields of cars for their events. They chose instead – with the blessing of the FIA – to run races counting for the World Championship according to the 2-litre Formula 2.

The BRM non-appearance at Turin in April 1952 was the final straw for the old Formula 1. Ferrari was present with three of its new 4½-litre cars for Ascari, Villoresi and the 1950 World Champion who had now joined the Maranello strength: Dr Giuseppe 'Nino' Farina. In practice Alberto complained about the 'hard and pointy' steering of his car. He also criticised the rear suspension, and when it was checked a fault was found and rectified.

In such matters he was reliable, said Aurelio Lampredi: 'There was no need for Ascari to have full engineering knowledge. He would either tell you "The rear suspension seems too stiff", or "That right-side tyre seems softer than the left", or "It's oversteering", or "It's understeering" – or sometimes, but rarely, "This engine's going to blow up." We'd check it out, find that he was nearly always right – and modify to correct accordingly.' Not detected at Turin, however, was a fault in the fuel tank that caused it to spring a leak when Ascari was in complete command of the race. When he ran out of fuel three laps before the flag the victory went to a surprised Villoresi.

Alberto Ascari raced this big Ferrari once more in 1952 and at an unfamiliar venue: Indianapolis. With its 4½-litre engine just right for Indy, the shrewd Enzo Ferrari succeeded in selling several cars to American racers. His cars' success in Mexico contributed strongly to their interest in buying a Ferrari. At the urging of his American agent Luigi Chinetti he also prepared a single entry to compete as a 'Ferrari Special' in the 500-mile race. Alberto Ascari underscored the exploratory nature of this expedition in May 1952:

'The *veni, vidi, vici* of imperial memory is not part of my spiritual baggage,' he joked. 'It seems to me I'm Christopher Columbus in miniature. I too am going to discover America. I'm going gladly, because I think that Indianapolis is an essential test for a good driver. If my experience there gives favourable results, the next year we'll return with a real team; only then could we conjure with dreams of victory. For the moment I'm a pioneer, going to learn.'

At Ferrari the driving force behind the project was Aurelio Lampredi. He had much greater confidence in the effort than he would allow his driver to reveal. Reliability was not expected to be a problem; the car had easily coped with 300 hard testing miles at Monza. Nor was the driver considered a liability. Enthusiast John Cuccio was among those who interpreted for Alberto, whose English was limited to 'Fine, fine'. Ascari easily passed his mandatory 'driver's test' and afterward pasted his three rookie-stripe tapes across the back of mechanic Stefano Meazza. 'When, at the conclusion of his tests, he was permitted some fast laps,' wrote Speedway expert Russ Catlin, 'American onlookers, in general, declared him a polished driver. There is no doubt that had his own car failed he could have had his choice of at least a dozen top-flight American cars to drive.'

Speed turned out to be the challenge. The Ferraris were lapping the 2½-mile track at no better than 132mph when the betting was that 135mph was needed to secure one of the 33 starting places. Testing was hampered by heavy rains during the week before the first qualifying weekend. More power was needed, and Lampredi thought he had the answer in Maranello. When he flew back from a quick visit his luggage contained a new inlet manifold with three four-barrel Weber carburettors. A bigger hood bulge was hammered out on the spot to make room for it.

'There were some truly great scenes to watch that year,' wrote Indy mechanic Clint Brawner. 'There was an Italian driver, Alberto Ascari, in a big Italian car, a screaming 12-cylinder Ferrari, who was downshifting for the corners four times per lap, yet turning identical lap times in spite of it.' This was amazing to the Indy regulars, who shifted only when they left the pits. Ascari went down a gear going into the pair of turns at each end of the lozenge-shaped track. Even so, the Ferrari seemed to lack the propulsive thrust out of the turns that the American cars enjoyed.

Finally, late on the last qualifying Saturday, the red number 12 Ferrari attempted to lap fast enough to make the grid. 'There has never been a four-lap qualifying run quite like Ascari's,' wrote Russ Catlin. 'The phenomenal thing was that in spite of shifting on each turn, Ascari turned in four laps that differed only eight hundredths of a second between the fastest and slowest. The third and fourth laps were made in identical time: one minute seven seconds flat! A Ferrari was in the race!' The speed was nothing special – 134.31mph in a field that averaged 135.50 – but it was sufficient. And Ascari's uncanny consistency created another legend of the Speedway. His successful qualification, with all the attendant Indy hoopla, 'was a very moving, unforgettable experience,' said Lampredi.

Ascari had reasons to hope for success. Unlike the Indy regulars, his crew had not used exotic fuels for qualifying, so his qualifying speed was also his potential race speed. Fuel economy was also an advantage. Before leaving Italy Ascari said he thought he could get through the 500 miles with only one stop for fuel. Instead tyre life was the limiting factor, so three stops were scheduled at 50-lap intervals to refuel and change tyres. 'The Americans were taking almost two minutes to refuel while we were taking 18 seconds,' said Lampredi. This would allow them to gain laps on the leaders.

'Alberto was to do the first section at 6,500 revs, then 6,500 again, then into the final offensive,' Lampredi added. 'So we thought we could win, with Alberto driving with his hands in his pockets. We were in for a surprise.' 'In the race I made the first laps at a reduced speed, wanting to study my opponents and the behaviour of our engine,' Ascari related. In Mexico he had competed against many of the leading American drivers, of whom he said, 'They are courageous and skilled, but they follow the theory "win or bust".' This could work in his favour at Indy.

Ascari: 'When I was persuaded I could throw myself forward, I accelerated from 21st up to seventh place.' Russ Catlin saw him make this move: 'The field was still bunched but, low and on the inside, came Ascari. He maneuvered past the field with a perfect exhibition of dirt-tracking. Some eyebrows were raised.' 'I now began to feel more at ease,' said the Ferrari driver, 'and to think that if bad luck did not pursue me, I might be able to arrive third or perhaps even second. I had already decided to wait for refuelling to make my offensive, when on lap 41 disaster struck.'

After three-quarters of an hour of racing the hub of Alberto's right rear wire wheel fractured. It broke partway between the splines that attach it and the rings of holes retaining the spokes. Feeling the wheel collapse in the fourth turn, he kept the red car under control as it swerved, veered into the infield and chuntered to a stop in the grass. Like Mauri Rose the year before, wire-wheel failure had stopped a contender, which was why most of the Indy regulars had already switched to magnesium wheels. 'He was out of the race,' wrote Catlin, 'but not until serving notice that he and his Ferrari are to be reckoned with, come another year. His performance, to this point, had been flawless.'

'He returned to the pits,' Lampredi related. 'He did not say a word for the rest of the race. Both our heads hung low that day, because we had had an easy victory in sight and we had lost our chance.' When he retired, before commencing his charge, Ascari had been averaging 128.71mph; the race winner averaged 128.92mph. Said American racing driver Sam Hanks, 'Ascari showed me enough in the 100 miles he lasted at the Indianapolis

500 to let me know he was equally at home on our speedway as on the road circuits of Europe. If he hadn't broken that wheel I firmly believe he would have had a lot to say at the finish.'

He might well have been in with a chance. His precise, decisive and consistent style was made to order for the Speedway. Thus the dark-suited Alberto commanded respect at the prizegiving dinner out of all proportion to the cheque for $1,983.19 with which he was presented for 31st place. That respect was underlined by the inscription on the back of an armband he was given by track officials: 'To Alberto Ascari – A Grand Guy'.

Following this glamorous and dramatic adventure the European season, with its many Formula 2 races, might have been an anticlimax, but Alberto Ascari made the most of it. By now he and Aurelio Lampredi were close collaborators. After winning at Monza in 1951 Alberto gave the engineer a photo with the following dedication: 'I am Ascari inasmuch as you are Lampredi. But you are Lampredi inasmuch as I am Ascari.' And for the 1952 season Lampredi had created a new 2-litre Formula 2 car, the Type 500, with a punchy four-cylinder engine, that was perfectly tailored both to the circuits and to his friend and star driver.

Nicknamed 'Starlet' by the Italian press in an allusion to its beauty, the new little Ferrari was destined to dominate the racing of the next two years. It was very capable, but driving it was no sinecure. British driver Roy Salvadori found that it was not 'particularly quick on the straight. It did not handle that well and was difficult to drift. There was absolutely no "feel" and it seemed to need a very precise driver; on the credit side it was beautifully built, it had excellent brakes and it was very reliable.'

Fortunately in Ascari it had just the driver required. Ferrari sold one of its 'Starlets' to French veteran Louis Rosier. In one of the early 1952 races at Marseilles Rosier was blaming the car for his inability to make the 500 go quickly. 'In front of everyone he spoke badly about our car,' Lampredi recalled. 'Therefore we made a rare decision in the history of motorsport and I asked Alberto, "Do me a favour. Would you mind testing this French gentleman's car? They are ruining our name, in front of the whole of Marseilles, in front of France." Alberto took that car and broke the track record!'

Over an S-bend on the Marseilles Parc Borély circuit,

hand timing revealed the relative performances of the drivers. Alberto was fastest at 5.2 seconds. The next group at 5.4 seconds included Farina and Villoresi. The dissatisfied Rosier required 5.6 seconds while some needed 5.8 seconds to negotiate the esses. The Ferrari had the driver it needed, as Lampredi remarked: 'Engines either run well or they break down. The only characteristic of a good racing engine is that it *never* breaks down. It *never* stops. This has always been my principle, but without Alberto that principle might never have been publicly affirmed.'

GP racing enjoyed two concurrent seasons in 1952. Seven races counted for World Championship points, with only the four best results being included. The French qualifying event at Rouen was also included in an all-French series of eight three-hour races for 18 designated cars and drivers from specific teams, points being awarded to both drivers and car marques. Ferrari won all the Grand Prix races, six of them with Alberto Ascari at the wheel. When he was away at Indy the Ferrari success in the Swiss GP went to Piero Taruffi. Ferrari also dominated the French series and Ascari its drivers' tally, although the honours there were more widely distributed.

Not that the 1952 European season began all that swimmingly in a March non-championship race. At the historic city of Syracuse a first-lap error by Alberto saw him smiting a hay bale and behind it part of a wall, which – being historic – obligingly gave way without damaging the Ferrari. Ascari was soon back in the lead and through the mid-race displayed his consistency with a string of identical fast laps.

Syracuse was the first victory in a season in which Ascari was overpowering. Gigi Villoresi took this philosophically: 'Justly, Alberto for Ferrari became number one both in his ability and with the friendship they had. They were very close, Alberto regarding Ferrari almost like a father and becoming something of a "spoiled child". This was then transmitted by Ferrari to his subordinates, such as [team manager] Nello Ugolini, to whose son Alberto became godfather. One of the secrets of a good start was to be considered as number one.'

Ferrari's favourite son won at Pau and then Marseilles in April. After his May sojourn in Indiana his first encounter with arch-rival Juan Manuel Fangio came at Monza in June. The Argentine was driving for Maserati, which had prepared a new twin-cam six-cylinder racer. While Ascari was on pole, Fangio started from the back of the grid, only having arrived on race morning after an all-night drive. Ascari won the first heat while Fangio crashed heavily on its second lap and was out of racing for the rest of the season. In the second heat of the June race Ascari broke a camshaft and the win went to Farina.

Also competing at Monza was Briton Peter Walker in an older V12 F2 Ferrari. Approaching Lesmo Corner, Walker spotted Ascari coming up behind to lap him. He decided that he was far enough ahead to be able to hold his line through Lesmo. 'I never lifted my foot,' Walker recalled. 'I just kept her going flat, and halfway through the corner Ascari goes by on the outside. I almost passed out in the cockpit.' Walker rallied to finish a fine fourth.

The second world-ranked race was at Spa, which – as so often – provided rain for race day. 'Ascari drove with exceptional regularity and complete superiority,' reported Rodney Walkerley, 'and his average varied by only 0.7mph from start to finish. Ascari finished all alone without a car in sight, touring over the line to stop at his pit instead of doing an extra lap and, as he switched off his engine, for several moments there was no sound of another car.'

Although Reims at the end of June did not count for World Championship points, any race at this historic circuit was important. Thus the French were entitled to leap for joy when ex-motorcyclist Jean Behra, in a new Gordini, moved into the lead and held it. Walkerley: 'Ascari tried every trick in his repertoire, but Behra, refusing to tow him in his slipstream, shook him off.' Alberto pitted for fresh plugs and Villoresi took over before handing the car back to Ascari for the final laps. They placed third.

A week later the French world-qualifying event was held at Rouen, where Ascari took pole position in spite of being completely new to the demanding road circuit. Said Rodney Walkerley, 'He was attacking that downhill swerve after the pits lap after lap until he could take it flat – at first with difficulty, but after a few more laps with what looked like ease – and chaps refused to believe it was possible after they had tried it themselves.'

From the race start, Walkerley continued, 'Ascari never lost his speed but increased it lap by lap, motoring faster and faster, his foot down where others lifted and flat out through curves which no others could take on full throttle. The works Ferraris once again demonstrated what fine cars they are on a normal give-and-take road surface and Ascari now leading for the World Championship underlines the fact that he is, with the possible exception of Fangio (still convalescing) the fastest driver in Europe today.' He won and set fastest lap as well.

Ascari next competed in one of the French championship races on his birthday, 13 July. Birthday or not, the 13th was not a lucky racing day, he pointed out after a spin by another competitor rendered his Ferrari unusable. He was fine, as he showed the next weekend by winning from flag to flag at Silverstone.

On the first weekend in August he seemed destined to do the same to win his third German GP on the trot until two laps before the finish when, wrote Rodney Walkerley, 'Drama reared its interesting head with its usual suddenness. Just as we sat back to watch Ascari tour round to win, he screeched to his pit in a ferment of agitation, covered in oil, to have a gallon or so slammed into the tail tank, looking back anxiously over his shoulder and unconsciously revving his engine to the red marks while he waited, a Prey to Apprehension. And lo, Farina sailed serenely by while Ascari bit his nails for 33 seconds.

'Now, with one lap to go, Ascari fought for his World Championship points,' Walkerley continued. 'He tore round that nightmare circuit, sliding the corners left and right, flogging the Ferrari to its limits. The crowds were on their feet shouting. Farina, unruffled and grinning, led before him, but with an ever-diminishing gap. Ascari had restarted with ten seconds to make up and in that one lap of fourteen miles he sliced it off until halfway round he was on Farina's tail, and he passed him in front of the roaring grandstand. Farina drew level again as they braked for the South Curve, but Ascari deftly swung his car through a tight sliding turn and led by a length out of the corner. So Ascari won his third post-war German Grand Prix – in spite of a fright.'

Ascari was tested again in the next race, the French-points Comminges GP. Steering trouble stopped his Starlet after two laps. Another works car was called in, André Simon ejected from it and Ascari installed. He quickly caught up all comers and won with a lap advan-

tage over team-mate Farina. At Zandvoort the next weekend for the Dutch world-points race 'Ascari electrified everyone in the practising by breaking all previous records for the circuit,' Walkerley reported. 'He lapped in 1min 48.4secs, 86.53mph on the first day and then slashed this to 1min 46.5secs, 92.402mph on the second, which was not only phenomenal but knocked 5.3 seconds off the existing lap record.

'As usual,' Walkerley added, 'practice showed inordinate tyre wear on this most abrasive of all circuits, and there was much anxious counting of spare tyres.' Alberto jumped into his customary lead. 'At half-distance, vast preparations were made in the pits to change all four of Ascari's wheels, but when they flagged him he waved them all aside and whistled by with a bland expression. He had taken a look at his wheels and felt happy, and on the 40 per cent methanol fuel he was using knew his mpg was adequate and next time round he lapped Villoresi and the pit pleaded with him to slow down.' Instead he set fastest lap on his way to victory.

Maserati was back for the Italian GP with the thrusting Froilán González on its strength. Starting with a half-full tank he took an early lead at Monza, but when he pitted Ascari flew by on a non-stop race to victory. González placed second and they shared the fastest lap, which meant that they had to split the single point. Thus Ascari's gross points tally for 1952 was 53½, of which he could count 36. Farina was vice-champion with 24 net points.

In a Ferrari Barchetta, joined by friend and champion motorcyclist Umberto Masetti, Alberto Ascari undertook a pleasant task during 1952. Masetti: 'We inaugurated Imola circuit, sharing the same car. It was a nice day. We were both World Champions but we weren't immoderately proud. Nevertheless the people cheering us made us understand that they felt our achievements were something of substance for our country.' Something of substance indeed.

Interest in Alberto Ascari and his Ferrari is tremendous at the Indianapolis Motor Speedway after his successful qualifying run on Saturday, 24 May 1952. He and his small crew pose for the official photographer while spectators gossip about a qualifying run that sets new standards for consistency.

Ferrari readies three of the most purposeful-looking racing cars ever made for the 1952 Formula 1 season. Ascari (left) and Nino Farina pose in theirs before the start of the Turin Grand Prix.

Alberto leads throughout the race (opposite and overleaf) but retires with a faulty fuel tank four laps from the finish. After Ferrari's abandonment of Formula 1 in 1952 he has few more chances to drive these great cars.

Ascari qualifies his Ferrari for the 1952 Indianapolis 500 (above), poses afterward with engineer Lampredi and mechanic Meazza (right), watches as Meazza and enthusiast John Cuccio push the Ferrari to its starting position on race day (below), and joins pith-helmeted Lampredi and white-suited veteran racer Ralph de Palma before the start (below right).

Although Ferrari considers his car's 1952 Indy entry to be 'unofficial', his prancing-horse emblem (omitted for qualifying) is restored for the race. Ascari astounds veteran race observers by speeding rapidly from 21st place to seventh before a right rear wire wheel fails and sends him ploughing into the infield grass.

An Ascari hallmark is his ability to leap immediately into the lead – usually from pole – to shrug off any challenge. In 1952 he demonstrates this in France at Sables d'Olonne on 13 July (opposite) and at Marseilles on 27 April (above) as well as in Britain at Silverstone on 19 July (bottom). He wins the latter two races but while leading at Sables d'Olonne is caught up in an incident with Harry Schell and suffers too much car damage to continue. Villoresi saves the day for Ferrari.

On this page clockwise from top left, Ascari is blessed as the best of the new generation by Tazio Nuvolari, jokes with Bindo Maserati, Mietta Ascari and Nino Farina's wife and a friend, spectates with Gigi Villoresi at Turin, and tries the cockpit of a rival Maserati with a sceptical look at that firm's

Guerrino Bertocchi. With mechanic Pasquale Cassani he grins at Rudy Mailander at Monza (opposite) and prepares to compete at Modena on the following weekend, 14 September. There he finishes third in the car of Sighinolfi (being flagged into the pits overleaf) after his own Ferrari succumbs.

Florists prosper in the Ascari years, a tradition that has to be given up when wreaths and bouquets start obscuring sponsors' patches on driving suits. Bouquets are in generous supply at Marseilles (above). Wreaths are the style at Silverstone (below) for Alberto and silver-haired second-place man Piero Taruffi. After winning at Rouen on 6 July (opposite left) he enjoys feminine attention and he raises his bouquet high after a satisfying victory in the Italian Grand Prix on 7 September.

The intensity of Alberto Ascari's concentration is evident as he corners on cobbles at Rouen (opposite) and Monza (above). Like his father, he prides himself on a precise knowledge of each circuit that allows him to utilise every opportunity it offers for quicker lap times. Clearly his time spent assessing the conditions before the race pays off the moment the starter's flag falls.

CHAPTER 6

Double champion

The cars built by Ferrari for the 1952 Carrera Panamericana were perhaps the most gorgeous and exotic sports-racing machines ever to leave the Maranello factory. Bodied by Vignale to a Michelotti design, they had aggressive looks that perfectly expressed the power of their 4.1-litre V12 engines. But 78 miles past the start of the race on 18 November Alberto Ascari's 340 Mexico coupé was looking decidedly second-hand. Taking a left-hand curve too fast – as the driver later admitted – the coupé left the road, rolled several times and smashed to a halt against an earth embankment.

This was an early end to another winter adventure in a sunny clime for Ascari. The Mexican campaign had again been undertaken by Milan's Scuderia Guastalla with three of the magnificent coupés, hoping to capitalise on the 1951 success. Alberto had been four minutes ahead of all rivals when he crashed – fortunately with only

After Ascari's victory in the 1953 Swiss Grand Prix Bernard Cahier captures his unique blend of pleasure in success and knowing self-deprecation. On this day, 23 August, Ascari seals his second World Championship with a dramatic fight from behind that had observers agog.

minor bruising thanks to a reinforced roof and his blue helmet. Testing and preparation had been inadequate, however, and the Ferraris succumbed to various ailments. One placed third behind two of the slower but steadier 300SL Mercedes. Alberto noted that the drivers had flown to Mexico on an unlucky Tuesday and suggested that a less-star-crossed day be chosen in future, even 'at the cost of swimming'.

Earlier in '52 Ascari had encountered the silver gull-wing Mercedes. At Le Mans he and Villoresi were given a 250S coupé, the Vignale-boded car with which Giovanni Bracco had beaten the 300SLs in the Mille Miglia. This was the progenitor of the great line of 3-litre V12 Ferraris. It was also a stunningly quick automobile. After the Thursday evening practice session Alberto told the team, 'This is the best car I have driven since I started racing.' He repeated this several times to be sure that they grasped his enthusiasm for the coupé.

Ascari's liking for the 250S showed in the speeds he achieved. Taking the Le Mans start, on the third lap he moved into the race lead. He led the field comfortably through the sixth lap but then pitted for attention to the clutch. Back in the race, Ascari demolished the lap record with a time of 4:40.5, even quicker than he had lapped in practice and equal to 107.59mph. After the first hour, however, the Ferrari had to be withdrawn. Such early retirements of the Ferraris at Le Mans were often blamed on the drivers, but in fact the cars sent by Maranello to the French classic were often inadequately prepared and tested by a company with a very hectic racing programme.

The Le Mans presence of Ascari, Villoresi and Ferrari was even more powerful in 1953. They arrived with an awesome Pininfarina-bodied 375MM coupé, its engine derived from that of Alberto's 1951 Formula 1 car. In practice Ascari lapped in 4:31, a speed of 112.61mph that Villoresi equalled during the race. Gigi took the first stint, dashing across the pit straight to leap into the coupé, which immediately became a contender for the lead.

Their chief rival turned out to be the C-Type Jaguar, which with its new disc brakes had a significant advantage. In the early-morning mist, said Jaguar driver Duncan Hamilton, 'I was never in danger of overshooting at Mulsanne while poor Ascari was obliged to brake early just to make sure.' Driving with Tony Rolt, Hamilton managed to maintain a two-lap lead over the Ferrari until, on the Sunday morning after three-quarters of a day of racing, the clutch that had worked for the Formula 1 Ferrari wilted under the weight of the heavier coupé.

Villoresi kept the Ferrari moving but it finally retired out on the circuit in the 19th hour. The Hamilton/Rolt Jaguar went on to win. 'Both Tony and I will always remember our dice with those two great Italians Villoresi and Ascari,' said Hamilton. 'In their refusal to give up while their car would still run they showed courage and determination of the highest order.'

They retired again in the Spa 24-hour race, this time while in the lead, with a failed final drive. At the end of August Ascari was paired with Nino Farina in a 375MM roadster to compete in the 1,000 kilometres of the Nürburgring. By bringing Ferrari a victory there the two World Champions contributed to the company's success in winning the 1953 World Sports Car Championship.

Twice in 1953 Alberto Ascari stepped back into the cockpit of the latest version of the 4½-litre 375F1 with which he had done so well in 1951. One was taken to Argentina at the beginning of the year to compete in an unrestricted race, but its oiling system misbehaved when Alberto was in the lead after setting fastest lap. Ferrari sent such a car for Alberto to Albi in France at the end of May to race against the supercharged BRMs in what was described as 'pitiless tropical heat which must be experienced to be believed.' Ascari, reported Rodney Walkerley, 'went off from as fine a commencement as I have ever seen, his tyres a blur of blue rubber-smoke … almost on fire'. After only three of the initial heat's ten laps, however, he retired with smoke coming from his gearbox instead.

A footnote to racing history was the entry for Indianapolis in 1953 of car number 97, an otherwise unidentified 'Ferrari Special' with a 3-litre supercharged V12 engine. Factory records show that this 250I engine developed 505bhp at 6,300rpm, which would have provided ample acceleration off the turns. Alberto Ascari was listed as the car's driver. That he fully expected the car to be made ready was shown by his rejection of the offer of a traditional Indy roadster by one of the leading entrants. Had Ascari materialised in Indy's Gasoline Alley in May 1953 he would have had no shortage of opportunities, even with his English limited to 'Fine, fine'.

In their World Championship season, again raced to Formula 2 rules, Ascari and Ferrari faced renewed competition from an again-healthy Fangio and cross-town rivals Maserati, their car tweaked for more speed by none other than Gioachino Colombo. Added interference came from the French Gordinis and British Coopers and Connaughts. As team-mates Alberto had Villoresi and Farina plus a tall, blond and British newcomer, the bow-tied Mike Hawthorn.

The winter warmth of Argentina was back on the 1953 calendar with the addition to the World Championship schedule of a Grand Prix at Buenos Aires. This was a triumph for Alberto Ascari, who won from pole with a fastest lap into the bargain, and a tragedy for GP racing and Perón's Argentina with multiple spectator fatalities after Nino Farina, swerving to avoid a youngster crossing the road, veered into the crowd. Bizarrely an ambulance racing to the scene also ploughed into the throng, causing further deaths.

Ferrari's European season began disastrously at Syracuse in March. All four Ferrari 'Starlets' retired with various problems, Mike Hawthorn's after Ascari took it over when his own car retired with engine trouble. For the next race at Pau on Easter Monday the works Maseratis were still not present so team manager Ugolini told his drivers to mix it up for the first two hours and then race for the final hour. After Farina spun off his remaining troops were Ascari and Hawthorn. Given free rein, wrote fellow competitor Harry Schell, 'Immediately Ascari leaps ahead and in five laps has a lead of 28 seconds over his team-mate Hawthorn – Ascari is really the finest driver I have ever seen.' In his winning drive he set fastest lap, the first ever to average faster than 100kph for the tortuous Pau circuit.

For the minor Bordeaux GP in early May Gigi out-qualified Alberto by a tenth of a second but the latter raced into an unchallengeable lead. At one-third distance Ascari had lapped 11 of the 15 runners, including Gordini-mounted Fangio. A week later the Argentine had a new Maserati for Naples, where he was still unable to challenge the Ferraris. Ascari lost many laps for a repair to his throttle pedal and finished only fifth.

June brought two world-points races in Holland and Belgium. Recently resurfaced and dusted with dune sand, the Dutch course was especially treacherous. Fangio challenged Ascari in qualifying but could not touch him in the race, which the Milanese dominated. The Maseratis were more of a threat at the fast Spa circuit, two of them joining Alberto on the front row of the grid. With half-full tanks they rushed away from the Ferraris, which were not stopping. González's Maserati set the fastest race lap its second time around.

'Ascari's handling was sheer artistry,' wrote John Cooper in *The Autocar*, 'but González, the fighter, seemed by brute force to make the car go where he wanted it; both methods were successful but Ascari's was the greater joy to watch.' Before mid-race both Maseratis were broken and Ascari drove through to victory, stopping immediately at his pit as he had in 1952. In fact since that race a year ago no-one else had won a championship Grand Prix (except for odd-race-out Indianapolis).

After Spa Alberto Ascari had won nine world-points races in a row, a quite staggering achievement that has not been equalled at the time of writing. If we take the Indy 500 into account his winning string ended after

seven races. His closest challengers have been Jack Brabham, Jim Clark and Nigel Mansell with five race wins in a row. He also broke all records by setting the fastest lap in six races in succession – all the 1952 races and the first of 1953. His nearest rivals have strung together only four fastest laps: Mansell again, Jackie Stewart and Gilles Villeneuve. Neither of these achievements by Italy's greatest racing driver of the modern era will easily be surpassed.

Ascari's sequence of championship GP victories was ended not by a member of a rival team but by a fellow Ferrari driver and a newcomer at that, Mike Hawthorn. At the fast Reims circuit the art of slipstreaming – conserving power by nestling in the wake of another car – could play a decisive role and so it was in July of 1953. The leading cars travelled in bunches and swapped positions so often that the lap chart looked like a cross-cut saw. 'At one point,' wrote Hawthorn, 'I passed Ascari and he shrugged his shoulders as if to say: "Take it away; I can't go any faster!"' Hawthorn ultimately won from Fangio in a race so close that the top six finishers were only 16 seconds apart; Alberto placed fourth.

This was one of the very few races in which Ascari, seemingly with healthy equipment, failed to match the performance of his rivals and indeed his team-mates. Enzo Ferrari famously remarked on this as follows: 'Alberto Ascari the driver had a sure and precise style, but Alberto Ascari the man had an impelling need to get into the lead at the very beginning. When leading, he could not easily be overtaken – indeed, I will go as far as to say that it was virtually impossible to overtake him. When he was second, however, or even further back, he had not the combative spirit I should have liked to have seen on certain occasions.

'This was not because he threw in the sponge;' Ferrari continued in his memoirs, 'but because, when he had to get on to the tail of an adversary and pass him, he was evidently afflicted not so much by what might perhaps appear to be a sort of inferiority complex as by a state of nerves that prevented him from showing his class to the best advantage. Ascari was just the opposite of what is generally the case: usually, in fact, it is the driver in the lead who is worried – he is harassed, he wonders whether or not he can hang on in the first place, he studies his pace and is often uncertain as to whether or not he should force it. With Alberto Ascari, though, it was exactly the contrary: he felt sure of himself when he was acting as the hare, and it was at those moments that his style was seen at its superb best and no-one could catch him.'

That Ferrari had fairly assessed Ascari in this respect was verified by motorcycle racer Umberto Masetti. 'Once he attended as a spectator a bike race in Monza, where I had problems at the start and I could only move off last,' Masetti said. 'But I didn't lose heart and sped off, riding my Benelli in pursuit of the 26 adversaries who went before me. I couldn't win but I arrived third, which was nonetheless a good result.

'After the race Alberto came to my pit to congratulate me,' Masetti added. 'He was astonished: "But how could you do that?" he asked. I answered that I was stimulated more and more by looking at the pit signals, which confirmed to me that I was gaining lap after lap. Alberto instead admitted that, when pursuing, his famous self-control was put to the test and his performance could scarcely reach 100 per cent. Basically he was worried, thinking that his efforts could prove to be in vain. And this could end up making him nervous or demoralised – a far cry from the strong self-controlled man he actually was.'

His rival Juan Fangio was all too aware of Alberto's intense drive to control the race from the front: 'Ascari was fast, terribly fast. He was a driver who gave great importance to practice times and starting in pole position. In this way he could be in front from the start and go out to win without anyone getting in his way. This method certainly worked, and he used it with monotonous regularity in the years when Ferrari dominated the World Championship for Formula 2.'

Asked how he got away from the start so quickly, Ascari said: 'The trick is to pull away immediately, at speed, without breaking the transmission. I do it almost instinctively. It's not something you can learn. Moreover, I study the track carefully before the race and try to make the most of it. Every circuit is different.' His strategy differed from race to race as well: 'It depends on my opponents. In short races it's often a good thing to let your rivals believe they have no chance whatsoever of beating you. In longer races, and therefore of greater endurance, it's best to let them believe they can win at the start.'

'Ascari always looked different from the other champions when he lined up at the start,' wrote Franco Bertarelli. 'He would slowly put his helmet on, tightening the buckle under his chin as calmly as dressmakers thread a needle, slide gently down into the cockpit and rest both hands on the steering wheel with muscles relaxed, in that "extended" driving position – with his body far away from the steering wheel – that was his characteristic.' Asked why he adopted that position, Ascari replied, 'I use what you would call the "long" style because it gives me greater freedom of movement and helps me keep my balance in corners. Moreover, by keeping my back against the seat, my hips "feel" the road-wheel action better.'

Although his position looked relaxed, giving him the scope he needed to manipulate the steering wheel with a vigour matched by few, Ascari poured all his energy into his races. 'For me a race is extremely tiring, exhausting,' he said. 'During the race it is thirst, above all, which torments you – a terrible thirst, which some men must quench during those three hours, thus forfeiting the race. I sweat so profusely in that boiling cockpit that I sometimes lose as much three to four kilos in weight. By the finish a bottle of ice-cold mineral water poured down my throat and down my neck and back is better than the finest Champagne in the world!' He would often have a swig of water and an impromptu shower during a pit stop.

When away from the races, said friend Mila Schön, Ascari 'was especially able to relax. When driving for touring he was incredibly laid back. Once we were driving back from Cortina to Milan and on a twisting mountain road he was driving very softly, without changing gear. So I asked him: "But perhaps you would arrive at Milan in fourth gear?" "Yes, I would," was the answer. And he did it! The *other* Alberto, the racing one, benefited from the relaxation he accumulated away from the tracks and put all his nervous energies into concentrating himself and all his strength on enduring the enormous fatigue of the race. Because racing then was a tiring job indeed!'

Belying his 'Ciccio' nickname, Ascari in fact was one of the few drivers who had a regular fitness regime. 'When Alberto was in training,' wife Mietta told Kevin Desmond, 'which was usually 11 out of 12 months of the year, he kept to an extremely healthy routine. For his daily exercise he would do gymnastics and jogging round the Velodromo Vigorelli, the world-famous bicycle arena near Corso Sempione. With this conscientious preparation he had an almost perfect physique. Often before he left for Argentina we would go to Cortina d'Ampezzo and enjoy some skiing. Then when he was in Belgium he and Nino Farina would play golf with King Baudoin and ex-King Leopold who were Ferrari enthusiasts – and when they came to Italy there would be a return match either at Monza or Rapallo golf course.'

'One of his fixations,' said racing driver Gino Munaron, 'was his alleged need to keep the speed of his reflexes in good shape. On a winter evening, with a thick fog, he would phone friend and photographer Corrado Millanta, inviting him to take part in a "training session". Corrado hadn't the courage to say "No", so he had to go. Once I was at Corrado's home when Alberto phoned, so the three of us had to go. Go where? The way wasn't too long: we went from Milan to Lodi and back, more or less 75 kilometres. But in that fog it looked like a nightmare. Alberto drove his Fiat 1900 and sped along regardless, just to train the speed of his reflexes. Corrado and I knocked on iron [not on wood, in Italy], but we could never refuse his invitations.'

'Although he was a great lover of food – pasta asciutta, risotto alla Milanese, French cheeses and pates, German wurst – his favourite food was beefsteak,' Mietta said, 'rare with eggs and a normal salad. He did not like curries and hot spicy dishes and preferred a good wholesome wine to an inebriating "shot". He hardly ever smoked. Every night he went to bed at 10:30pm, glanced at the newspapers and exactly at 11 o'clock he would fall asleep. He would, if possible, get up late and take his time to wash, shave and dress, which he did – as he did most things – very meticulously. I once referred to him as a methodical bourgeois husband.'

Both meticulousness and superstition continued to regulate Ascari's life. Gigi Villoresi gave an example: 'We had two boxes where we kept our helmets, goggles, gloves, etc. They were both painted azure blue. Nobody – not even Mietta – was allowed to touch Alberto's box except himself. One day he was out lapping in the Ferrari and I had need of a little piece of white cotton wool to put in my ears, because in those days we did not have noise-padded helmets and I had forgotten to bring my own. So I opened his box. On top was a pair of gloves which I moved ever so carefully. Then I took a little piece of cotton wool. Then I put everything back *exactly* as I had found it. He stopped at the pits, opened his box and said, "Hey! Who's been mucking about with my things?" Obviously I had put those gloves back two millimetres out of place, no more.'

Undeterred by the nightly visitations of a cat to the landing outside his hotel room, or indeed by a late-race thunderstorm – and never headed by those pesky Maseratis – Alberto Ascari returned to his winning ways by leading from start to finish in the British GP at Silverstone in mid-July of 1953. 'Ascari's drive was so perfect that his polished skill almost passed unnoticed,' wrote Rodney Walkerley, 'until it was observed that he was two laps ahead of Farina, no slow coach and on a similar machine, running non-stop likewise.'

At the Nürburgring in August Alberto seemed set fair to win his fourth German GP running, recording the only lap time under ten minutes in practice and bettering it in the race. 'During the first few miles,' wrote Mike Hawthorn, 'he nearly rammed Fangio as he braked for the corners with smoke pouring from the car' before taking the lead. To his mechanics' surprise, however, he ended his fifth lap by coasting into his pit minus a right front wheel. 'How the dickens he kept the car on the road,' wrote Walkerley, 'slumped sideways in front at about 150mph, took it something over a mile up a hill and round two curves to pull up gently just past the pits, is, we thought, more a demonstration of his mastery than even the way he had been galloping away from the rest of the race.' Later he switched to Villoresi's car but this broke its motor and Ascari had to retire.

Three weeks later the Swiss GP at Berne could settle the World Championship, which Alberto was leading handsomely in spite of his German retirement. He led as usual from the front row but his engine began to misfire and on the 40th of 65 laps he stopped for 88 seconds' worth of carburettor repairs. This dropped him to fourth but after a Maserati retired he was third behind Hawthorn and Farina.

'Even finishing third,' said Ferrari mechanic Ener Vecchi, 'Alberto was sure to clinch his second World Champion title. So team manager Ugolini ordered chief mechanic Meazza to show the three Ferrari drivers a blue-yellow flag, meaning "Hold your positions". But Ascari didn't obey, performing instead a fantastic pursuit, catching Hawthorn and Farina and overtaking them to arrive first once again.' His determination to clinch the championship had helped him overcome his reluctance to challenge from behind. Farina, who had been leading, was anything but pleased and said so to Ascari, who protested that the low sun at Berne had blinded his view of the 'keep stations' flag.

Rodney Walkerley celebrated Ascari's achievement: 'You know, he is a most astounding driver. He rarely appears to be motoring in a hurry until you watch very closely on the faster curves, whereupon it becomes clear that if he is lifting his foot at all, it is much later than anyone else – and we mean, anyone – or just not lifting his foot. One has only to regard the fact that he had four seconds lead after four laps over Fangio, who is no sluggish motorist, and 20 seconds over Farina.'

The Ferrari team's atmosphere was still stormy when the racers foregathered for the last points race of the year at Monza in September. This developed into a breathtaking display of slipstreaming among Ascari, Farina and Fangio. On the last turn of the last lap Alberto was leading when they encountered a slower Maserati. Ascari: 'I decided to throw myself towards the outside of the track. The opening was very narrow. In a flash I saw clearly that I would not succeed in passing. But I wanted to risk it in spite of everything. When you race 500 kilometres as important as Monza and are so close to success it is impossible to hesitate in front of danger. It is perhaps a madness, a useless risk, but one feels the right and almost the duty to try.

'So at 105mph I attempted the narrow outside passage,' Ascari continued. 'The track was streaked with oil. My Ferrari skidded sideways. Farina, just behind me, braked and swerved. He lost precious time and Fangio, who was third, succeeded in sliding between us and winning. I had never lost a race in the final metres. It is a thing that stings, especially if you think that I had led the race for the last 27 laps and previously for another 32. But then it *was* the 13th of the month.'

Monza had been unkind to Ascari earlier in the year. On the 13th lap of a sports-car race at the end of June he was driving a Ferrari roadster that suddenly had a control failure. 'I distinctly remember only that the car, going through the bushes, moved zigzag for 60 metres, jumping up and hitting the shrubbery,' he recalled. 'Next I found myself standing up. My first reaction was to shake arms, legs and feel my thorax to persuade myself that I was whole. No injuries at all. Friends who had witnessed the accident told me that they had seen me literally flying out of the car and falling heavily on the ground. Personally, I had the impression of being in my seat up to the last moment and of coming out of my car when it stopped. But the film of that race showed my car after the accident with upturned wheels in the air – proving my friends to be right.'

The image of an overturned Ferrari became graphically symbolic in the days before the Italian GP at Monza. At the end of August, said Mike Hawthorn, 'the newspapers carried startling stories to the effect that Ferrari had decided to give up motor racing. He pleaded that he was tired and needed a rest; he was known to be worried about his son, who suffered from chronic ill-health, and he even alleged that one of his draughtsmen had been smuggling drawings out of the factory for use by his rivals.' The real reason, of course, was that Ferrari was concerned – and rightly – about the challenge from Mercedes-Benz and, reportedly, Lancia and Alfa Romeo, in the new 2½-litre Formula 1 coming in 1954.

Yet did Ferrari not have all the equipment needed? Had he not dominated the years that were effectively a preview of the next Formula? Had he not shown a squat, purposeful new GP car, the latest Lampredi creation, before Monza? And had the double World Champion, Alberto Ascari, not posed for photographers at the wheel of this very car? And were the personal and professional bonds between Ferrari and Ascari not very strong? All these things were indeed so, promising an excellent start to the 1954 season for Ferrari and Ascari. How deceptive expectations can be.

Rudy Mailander captures the start at Le Mans in 1952 as Alberto Ascari, near a small white fence, prepares to run to the 250S Ferrari that he considers the best racing car he has yet driven. Before clutch failure he shows his heels to two Mercedes-Benz 300SLs, one of which will win the race.

Before Le Mans in 1952 Alberto's attention is drawn to a technical point by Charles Faroux (above left). Uncharacteristically driving-suited (above right), he responds to a question from Mailander.

On a hot day at Monza Alberto tests his Ferrari Le Mans mount for 1953 (below left). After the Casablanca 12-hour race at the end of 1953 in which he and Villoresi finish second, Ascari is joined by bobble-hatted winner Nino Farina.

At Monza in June 1953 Ascari's new Ferrari sports-prototype leaps into the lead ahead of two Lancia roadsters. Overtaking a lapped car at the Lesmo corner, he suffers a control failure and a heavy crash that throws him from the overturning Ferrari. The 735S is a precursor of the 750S Ferrari in which Ascari is killed in a strikingly similar accident on the next turn of the same track two years later. Ascari checks the sporting news at Monza (overleaf) during pre-Le Mans tests and leads the Jaguars of Stirling Moss (17) and Tony Rolt (18) at Le Mans, a battle that continues until the Ferrari finally succumbs.

Among Ascari's rivals only Fangio is able to match him in the art of starting a race. He does so in his BRM in the spectacular start at Albi on 31 May 1953 (left) and at the Nürburgring on 2 August 1953 (above). Following Fangio (5) and Ascari (1) through the South Turn are Hawthorn, de Graffenried, Bonetto, Trintignant, Villoresi and eventual winner Farina. Alberto leads from the start (overleaf) to win the Grand Prix of Argentina on 18 January 1953.

After his race at the 'Ring in 1953 Ascari walks to the paddock with his precious kit. At Pau on 6 April 1953 he shortens the snout of his Ferrari during practice. His 'Starlet' is repaired in good time for the race, which he wins while setting fastest lap (opposite).

Alberto Ascari and the Type 500 are a formidable combination in 1953. He drives Villoresi's car to eighth place at the Nürburgring after his own fails (left) and wins at Berne, here heading Fangio and Hawthorn (above). Clockwise from top left on the opposite page, he charges to victory in Argentina, Silverstone, and Berne, and leads until losing a wheel at the Nürburgring.

With Lampredi, a tweedy Alberto attends to the views of mechanic Meazza (top left). Ascari thinks highly of new British team mate Mike Hawthorn (top right). He gestures vigorously

to make his points at the Nürburgring (bottom left and right). Ascari is joined by Lampredi at Berne in 1953 (opposite), where he wins in the car created for him by the engineer (overleaf).

CHAPTER 7

Spear carrier

Ascari had one more burden to bear. Nuvolari was dead. He died on 11 August 1953. Alberto shed tears over the passing of a great man who was an important link with his father and who had gone out of his way to commend the efforts of the son. He travelled to Mantua to help support Nuvolari's coffin with his shoulder. Now the modest Ascari could not escape the realisation that he stood alone as the idol of millions at the very apogee of his sport.

Among Italians, of course, adulation of Ascari was unbounded. As an Italian sportsman he was famed and honoured on the same supreme level as Fausto Coppi, the country's legendary champion cyclist. Born the year after Alberto, Coppi was linked with the driver in his use of Bianchi bicycles for many years. In 1949 he was the first-ever cyclist to win the Giro di Italia and the Tour de France in the same year. His career included five wins of the former and two of the latter. In 1953, contemporane-

It is half past two on a warm afternoon at Reims on 4 July 1954 and Alberto Ascari is about to take the start in a Maserati 250F. That he retires on the second lap will be only one of the many frustrations he must suffer in this difficult season while awaiting his new Lancia.

ously with Ascari's second championship, Fausto won the World Road Racing Championship. Coppi and Ascari were friends who, when holidaying and relaxing together, could compare notes on the benefits and burdens of fame.

Ascari's astonishing string of victories in 1952 and '53 was described as a 'triumphal march'. Yet the man was not ideally equipped to relish his nation's fervent adoration. Wrote Piero Casucci, 'We admired in Alberto Ascari not only the serious and conscientious athlete but also the anti-star who even shunned the wave, the cheers of the crowd at the end of his many victories. When he did wave – rarely – it was in an ironic style.' His most vigorous and sincere gestures to the crowd came only after those races that had fulfilled his rigorous personal standards for success, such as the 1951 German Grand Prix.

'He wasn't a good public relations man for himself,' said Mila Schön. 'Sometimes he could seem to keep new acquaintances at a distance. It took him a certain amount of time to get familiar with somebody.' 'He hated journalists who pestered him, interviewed and then went away and wrote what they wanted,' his wife recalled. 'He didn't like people taking advantage of his friendship, who only wanted to meet him so that they could say they were "friends" with the great Alberto Ascari.'

Driver Gino Munaron confirmed that Ascari 'wasn't eager to make new acquaintances. He was very satisfied with his family and his group of friends. He was shy. And sometimes his behaviour could be that typical of every shy guy: his reactions could seem to be aggressive. When he was at his ease he was a jolly companion, amused and amusing with his pleasantries, laughing and entertaining. But when new people joined the group, Alberto was very self-controlled. Sometimes he could cut himself off. His behaviour was influenced by the two main impulses that drove him: the unforgettable loss of his father and his great sense of responsibility as a father as well as a racing driver.'

Ascari sought always to be true to those responsibilities, Gilberto Colombo recalled: 'I think that my friend Alberto Ascari realised that as a World Champion it was his duty to be an exemplary Italian citizen. I even remember his making a broadcast about road safety on the newly-born Italian television. When crossing a city he drove calmly and respectfully, always on the lookout for wobbling cyclists or careless pedestrians. He often changed his personal car, saying that a car must always be new and well kept. Once on the Autostrada or main roads he went extremely fast, but engendered in his passenger a sense of absolute security.'

Corrado Millanta gave an insight into such a trip from Milan to Genoa. 'He came to get me in his Aurelia Gran Turismo.' The journalist recalled. 'The main road at that time started at Serravalle and had only one lane. On the initial downhill stretch that ended in a sharp left-hand turn that led onto a bridge he told me to watch the way he would get the car to "move out". We turned into the bridge at around 85mph and the Aurelia promptly "moved out". He did not allow it to get sideways. Elegantly correcting – I can still see his right hand looking like that of a violinist holding his bow – he said to me, as if we were talking about nothing in particular, "See, Mr Millanta?" "I see," I replied and thought – I who had been thinking about taking part in a race one day – that it would be best if I collected stamps.'

Ascari's sense of responsibility toward his family, especially his two young children, was strong. They continued to live at Corso Sempione 60, where, wrote

visitor Günther Molter, 'a bronze bust of Antonio Ascari on a simple wooden plinth graces the entrance hall, erected by a thoughtful son to the memory of an unforgettable father. Daylight is almost excluded from this hall and the bust stands there in semi-darkness as if in the solitude of a chapel. The street noises hardly penetrate here, nor does the heat of the Italian summer. On the first floor a simple wooden door bears a brass plate – Alberto Ascari.'

Life behind that door was placid, quiet, conventional. 'Ascari spent his private life, mainly thanks to his wife Mietta, in a peaceful environment,' wrote Franco Bertarelli. 'He was particularly fond of dark double-breasted suits. He played golf dressed impeccably, without bright coloured jumpers, calm, confident, friendly and elegant. A man who drove his saloon car gently with a beautiful family at his side, with an air that surpassed affluence: this is the impression he gave to those who did not know him.'

'He was a quiet man with a kind and friendly face,' said Villoresi. 'Neither his appearance nor his manner revealed a champion at first sight. He was level-headed and very rational. He had great determination both in life and his races. Order and precision were the key words: he looked like an old accountant. And he often told me off for being untidy. "Basically he's just a methodical bourgeois," his wife Mietta used to say, laughing. "He always gets annoyed if he finds anything out of place."'

'At home,' said Mietta, 'one did not speak about motor racing. When he was away racing he often telephoned me, but we chatted about banal things, about the children, the weather, about whether I was going out or staying in – for he became very jealous of me when he was not home. When he returned from abroad he would bring back precious and semi-precious stones saying, "Furs will lose their value. These won't." For the children mechanical toys and toy cars came from Germany for Tonino, while at Reims in France they made special dolls, in a different costume each year, for him to bring back to Patrizia.'

'I usually try to give my children everything they need – even if it is only to satisfy a whim,' Ascari admitted. Nevertheless he felt that he needed to be relatively stern and distant: 'I think it as well that I should be severe with them. I don't want them to get too fond of me. One of these days I may not come back. They will suffer less if I have kept them at arm's length.' Umberto Masetti observed this behaviour by his friend: 'It is true that his attitude with his children was less tender and affectionate than one could imagine. I perfectly understand it. This is my way and it was Alberto's too.'

Reports of Ascari's sternness with his family may be exaggerated, however. 'He could only stay with us for two months more or less per year,' recalled son Tonino, 'because his racing commitments kept him elsewhere for the other ten months. Thus he could not be too severe a father. I don't remember him inflicting punishment. Sometimes he was preaching, like most parents normally do. He hadn't been a model student, so when I got bad marks or played truant he said something to me, of course, but smiling ...'

Left with the children for the other ten months of the year, Mietta Tavola Ascari was in fact the person who had to impose discipline: 'I was more strict with the children than he was, because when he was at home – which was seldom – he gave them everything they wanted. Then he went off again and I would have to regain control of them. But neither Tonino nor Patrizia ever went to see their father race.'

Life on the Corso Sempione was comfortable but not lavish. Ferrari relied on his share of starting and prize money to keep his company afloat and was not minded to be overly generous with his drivers. 'Alberto did not think that Ferrari paid him well enough for his successes,' Mietta said. 'If he won a Grand Prix half went to Ferrari and half went to Alberto – 500,000 lire each. However, the cycling champions received 4 million lire for every race they won. A soccer player was paid even more. He was not paid in relation to the risks he took. Whenever I said I didn't like what he was doing he would reply, "This is my job" and I would reply, "Yes, but rather too dangerous a job, so why don't you consider changing it?"'

Ascari did in fact consider doing just that. One of his uncles had taken over the Fiat dealership under the flat on Corso Sempione and had been running it for many years as his own, without reference to Antonio's widow. 'I tried to convince him to work with his uncle,' Mietta recalled. 'The proposition was that Alberto would become partners with his uncle's son Ezio and they would do the agency work together.'

In 1954, well into his thirties, Ascari was prepared to consider such an arrangement. When alerted accordingly the uncle was suddenly less amenable: 'Perhaps not, Alberto, for I have looked after this agency for 25 years. It is mine and I want to go on with things the way they are. If you want to come and work here, you can be a salesman.' Not one to be bullied, Ascari replied, 'No, thank you. I'd prefer to continue racing.' Mietta: 'Afterward his uncle regretted his offer because if he had made Alberto a partner everyone would have gone to that agency hoping to find Alberto Ascari there.'

In his current profession, of course, double champion Alberto Ascari was a hot property. Among racing-car builders gearing up for the launch of the new Formula 1 in 1954 he could expect to be in intense demand. In the meantime he was still under contract to Ferrari; in fact the current contract did not expire until the end of April 1954. But was Ferrari intending to race? The uncertainty that had lingered since the mutterings about withdrawal in August was not dissipated until 12 December, when Enzo Ferrari held his season-ending dinner. He would compete in the major events, he said, while at the same time bemoaning the lack of support he was receiving from the infrastructure of the nation whose prestige he was upholding internationally.

Enzo Ferrari's prolonged sulk meant that his engineers were less advanced than they might have been in their preparations for 1954. 'They wouldn't tell us what we would be doing in 1954,' Villoresi said. 'They produced no programmes and said not a word, causing us to waste a lot of time.' Plans for 1954 were to be the subject under discussion when Alberto and Gigi travelled to Maranello for a meeting on Tuesday, 29 December. While Villoresi chatted with team manager Ugolini, Ascari sat down with Ferrari in the monastic cell that served as his office.

After their opening pleasantries Ferrari startled the driver with his request. 'Ascari,' he said, 'by 1 January I'd like to renew your contract that expires on 30 April 1954. Do you agree to continue racing for me? I'd like an immediate reply. If you do choose to accept would you please sign the contract immediately?' Alberto had neither anticipated this request nor did he know why

Ferrari had arrived at this 'extreme measure'. The car maker, aware of the attraction that Ascari held for other teams, may have wished to lock up his talented champion for the full year while denying him four additional months during which others could treat for his services.

Ascari recalled the scene: 'I replied: "Listen, Ferrari, I've also had very favourable offers from other constructors. I may still race for you if you are able to wait until 30 April. However, if you were to force me to come to a decision here and now, I must refuse your offer." He answered that he couldn't wait. So I did not sign. I returned to Milan the same evening with a sad heart. I had made too many sacrifices for the house of Maranello and the collaboration had given me too much satisfaction to be able to close a chapter as passionate and as attractive in my life without having some regrets, some nostalgia.

'The evening of 29 December,' Ascari continued, 'I closed the door of my study to examine the various propositions which had been made to me. I had received several from both Italian and foreign companies. Excellent, serious, concrete offers. The following day, in the morning, I left for Turin with Gigi Villoresi, destination Lancia. Gianni Lancia and I had known one another for many years. Every time we met I would ask him, "Well, then, when will you decide to build a racing car?" to which he always replied, "As soon as I have a little time!" At Turin that morning we told Gianni Lancia that we had left Ferrari. Gigi and I were free. If we could be useful we were at his disposal. Lancia replied, "Okay, now we'll see what we'll decide to do. But I feel sure that something good will come of it."'

This sudden act, this quick trip down the Autostrada to Turin to see the man whose family owned the Lancia motor works, was not the most obvious step for the serious, loyal, thoughtful Alberto Ascari to have taken. 'In fact,' he said afterward, 'I'll go as far as to say that I'd almost definitely have signed my contract with Ferrari again on 30 April. However, after what happened at Modena, I felt I was free to act as I deemed appropriate. And that's what I did.'

At 5:15pm on 30 December 1953 the Ferrari press office released a communiqué stating: 'Effective 31 December the existing collaborative relationship with the racing driver Alberto Ascari will cease.' It went on to claim that the 'sole reason' for this was Ascari's desire to orient his activities more commercially for the sake of his family and – in a manner inconsistent with the facts – attributed the schism to Ferrari's inability to offer his driver the rewards that other motor companies could provide. This was true enough, but as we have seen it was not the prime cause of the year-end break in relations.

All Italy – and much of the rest of the world of motorsports – was aghast at the news of the divorce. 'I never imagined my name would have caused such a stir,' said the modest Alberto. 'I thought the papers would only talk about the Ascari Lancia–Ferrari affair for a day or two. They went on for a lot longer.' For Italy, Ferrari and Ascari had become as inseparable as Verdi and La Scala. What did it mean?

The drivers' visit to Lancia was publicly known, but the Turin firm had not yet disclosed its Grand Prix programme. Would driving Lancia's sports cars be enough for Ascari? After reviewing these issues *Auto Moto Sport* wrote, 'The sole certainty – and not a happy one – is that the glorious Ferrari–Ascari binomial, which was able to bring two World Championships to our banner, has been definitively severed. It is this, we think, that will be a source of regret for all real sports fans.'

Mutual friends had helped prepare the ground for the link with Lancia, which was in fact readying a Formula 1 car. The decision to build it had been taken in the summer of 1953 and the drawings had been completed by a team under Vittorio Jano – the same Jano who had designed Alfas for Antonio Ascari – on 14 September. Before his death at the wheel of a Lancia sports-racer in the Carrera Panamericana at the end of 1953, Felice Bonetto had strongly recommended to Gianni Lancia that he engage Ascari's services. This generous driver had made the same recommendation to Enzo Ferrari in 1949. Six years younger than Alberto, the tall, burly Lancia was eager to move his company into the modern era with a successful Grand Prix car.

Lancia's winning performance in Mexico had appealed to Alberto: 'The enthusiasm with which Lancia faced a very hard and demanding race full of unexpected occurrences such as the Mexican Carrera greatly influenced my decision. He handled it with a great deal of spirit and courage and perfect organisation. A driver is won over by such things.' Thus he became a spear-carrier – *lancia* meaning 'lance' or 'spear' in Italian.

The liaison with Lancia was logical, Mietta Ascari said: 'Alberto had built up a great friendship with Gianni Lancia over the years and the transition was very natural. Lancia was very enthusiastic about his new car; he couldn't wait for it to be tested by a driver like Alberto. And he offered Alberto and Villoresi such favourable conditions that they both accepted immediately.' 'Lancia offered Ascari an opportunity not to be missed,' said Romolo Tavoni. 'With Ferrari, Alberto earned more or less 10 million lire per year, while with Lancia that sum rose to 25 million. Besides, there was the benefit of a Lancia B20 permanently in Alberto's garage.'

Their relationship was formalised on Wednesday, 20 January 1954, when both Alberto and Gigi signed contracts with Lancia. With and without designer Jano they were photographed on the Thursday next to a one-tenth-scale model of the new GP car, the existence of which was thus acknowledged for the first time. The next week found them in San Remo with Taruffi for tests of the Lancia sports-racers which were entered at Sebring in March. The GP car would be ready to race by June, Ascari hoped: 'If so I will be in time to dispute the last seven races for the World Championship. The Dutch or Belgian Grand Prix could see the baptism of this car.'

On 20 February, at Turin's Caselle Airport, Ascari drove the new Lancia D50 for the first time after it was shaken down by company tester Giuseppe Gillio. It was a symbolic occasion that marked the beginning of an arduous natal phase for this radical racer, built by a company that had never before made a single-seater racing car. It was destined to take longer than Ascari expected.

In the meantime there were sports-car races to run for Lancia – although fewer than planned, as the company concentrated its resources on the GP car project. A four-car team of maroon D24 racers was shipped to Sebring, Florida, where all suffered various ailments. The Ascari/Villoresi car lasted only into the fifth of the 12 hours. The Mille Miglia in May would have been off limits for Ascari had he not been acquitted, while away in Florida, of the manslaughter charge arising from his 1951 crash. When Villoresi was injured in a practice crash 13 days before the race Alberto suddenly found himself assigned to the Lancia Mille Miglia strength.

'Right from the start Taruffi led the race in a 3.3 Lancia, drawing gradually away from an unusually cautious Ascari,' *The Motor* reported. 'Among the Abruzzi Mountains on the way to Rome, Taruffi's oil pressure began to flicker but, driving at terrific speed, he came in the Rome control leading Ascari by four and a half minutes and then stopped to rectify the fault and lost the best part of an hour, and Ascari shot off into the lead on the return half of the long race which has always been the decisive stage. It is an axiom: who leads at Rome loses the Mille Miglia.'

On the way north Alberto's throttle return spring failed and was temporarily replaced by a rubber band. This and other problems were assailing his D24, said Aston Martin's John Wyer: 'I saw Ascari at the Florence control and he was in terrible trouble and ready to quit. Only after a long stop was he persuaded to carry on to Bologna, where Lancia had a depot.' A change in the route brought the competitors through Mantua in honour of Tazio Nuvolari. Bystanders saw Ascari salute the great lost driver as he passed the grey-marble cemetery lining the right side of the road.

By setting the fastest time from Cremona to Brescia through Mantua, Ascari won the Nuvolari Trophy that year. He also won the Mille Miglia, averaging 86.72mph. 'Let it be clear,' he said after the race, 'that this victory I owe, before everything else, to the advice given to me by Biondetti – advice which I have treasured.' Living on the course near Florence, Clemente Biondetti had won the race four times. His advice to Alberto? It was, wrote Kevin Desmond, 'that he would only win this race by prudence and by sustaining the courage and determination, despite fatigue, to keep his foot *off* the accelerator.'

At the end of June Alberto went to Portugal to drive in the Oporto Grand Prix for sports cars. He led until retiring on the 38th of 45 laps, spinning after a tyre burst. Villoresi was the winner, followed by new Lancia man Eugenio Castellotti. His only other drive in a sports Lancia was in September in the Tourist Trophy, run as a 700-mile handicap race over Northern Ireland's daunting Dundrod road course.

Although Ascari was the first to get inside the five-minute mark in practice and was timed at 144.6mph over Dundrod's flying kilometre, in the race Hawthorn's new Ferrari Monza could just match him for speed. They had a needle match for the lap record which the Briton finally won. During his final stint, Hawthorn wrote, Ascari 'had a narrow escape from serious injury, as the propeller shaft broke and tore through the centre tunnel within inches of his thigh.'

What else did an underemployed racing driver do during the summer of '54? Alberto and Gigi amused themselves by turning up at Monte Carlo for the filming there of a fake sports-car race for the film *The Racers*, also known as *Such Men Are Dangerous*. Encouraged to take part by driver Louis Chiron, they pocketed an extra 30,000 francs a day for hippodroming around parts of the road circuit, even using a D24 Lancia. Ascari also brought one of the Lancias, equipped with a special full-width windscreen, to Campione in Switzerland for the annual race-driving school.

They also managed some Grand Prix racing. Gianni Lancia organised two 250F Maseratis for his drivers for the French GP at Reims, where Alberto placed his on the front row of the grid next to the two Mercedes of Fangio and Kling. 'After the pits at Reims,' wrote Denis Jenkinson, 'there is a long right-hand curve approached at something like 140–150mph over a blind brow and on his fast lap Ascari took this without lifting his foot, something which no-one else had done, even Fangio lifting on the Mercedes-Benz, though he was probably going faster.' In the race Ascari's challenge failed with his engine on the second lap.

Alberto and Gigi were entered by the Maserati works for the British GP, later in July. There they had a distinct sense of *déjà vu*, for as in 1948 their Maseratis arrived so late that they had to start from the back of the grid. This time, however, there was no immediate leap to the front. 'Ascari quickly mounted to sixth place,' reported Rodney Walkerley, 'fell to last after a pit stop and then had valve trouble. Taking over Villoresi's car in seventh place he kept it there for a few more laps and then that engine, too, came to rest in clouds of smoke. He reputedly enquired at the pits: "Any more Maseratis?"' He shared fastest lap with six other drivers in an era when the British timed to the nearest second.

An Italian Grand Prix in 1954 without Alberto Ascari? Certainly not. But for this he made a one-off return to the Scuderia Ferrari that hinted at what the 1954 season might have been like had he remained at Maranello. Although Fangio secured pole position in his Mercedes, Alberto was only a fifth of a second away with a time set at the very end of practice. *The Autocar*: 'He went round (in a very frightening fashion on the Lesmo and South corners) in 1m 59.2s, just one-tenth of a second faster than Moss and sufficient to earn him the headlines in all the late evening and morning papers – and the second of the two practice-day prizes.'

Unused to the Ferrari, Ascari was slow away, but on the sixth lap he took the lead from the hated Mercedes of Fangio: 'He is the Italian hero,' Walkerley reported, 'and the crowd went mad, all 85,000 of them cheering themselves hoarse. Down the straight Ascari and Fangio raced side by side, three feet apart, until one gave way into the next curve, but at 23 laps Fangio held on, slipped ahead and led by a length. Next lap Ascari did the same and led the Mercedes, lapping at nearly 115mph. On lap 45 Moss passed [Ascari] and a British driver led the Italian Grand Prix averaging 112.72mph, but Ascari re-passed using we suspect over-advanced rpm. Next lap they were side by side on the straights, nose to tail on the corners, and then Ascari's engine gave up. Moss flew past him looking back with some concern, Ascari shrugged and two laps later retired.'

For the first time in 1954 the reigning World Champion had led a Grand Prix race, and had done so decisively – as was his style. Would Lancia produce a car worthy of his skill? There was still time in 1954 to find out.

Lancia team manager Attilio Pasquarelli proudly bears the precious blue helmet ahead of his leather-jacketed driver, winner of the 1954 Mille Miglia. Wrote The Autocar, *'Ascari's big lead made it possible to announce him as the winner immediately on arrival, for no competitor starting after him had a hope of catching him on the last leg. The scene of enthusiasm on Ascari's arrival at Brescia was indescribable, and crowd control almost impossible; but, remarkably, no accidents occurred.' The faces in the crowd give ample evidence of the pleasure that fellow Italians take in this fine victory by Alberto Ascari.*

One of Alberto Ascari's first tasks on joining the Lancia team at the beginning of 1954 is to assist in its tests of the D24 sports-racing car at San Remo on 8–9 February. He discusses the tests with Gianni Lancia and hatted team manager Pasquarelli and takes his seat in the D24 watched by works tester Gillio. For more tests at San Remo in December 1954 Alberto joins and jokes with (opposite, left to right) test driver Giuseppe Navone, Vittorio Jano, Gigi Villoresi, and chief timer Motto. There were not too many happy times that season.

The strong Lancia effort at Sebring on 8 March 1954 – Ascari and Fangio are on the same team – is blunted by mechanical failures (opposite).

Although suffering various vicissitudes, Ascari's D24 Lancia travels victoriously from start (above) to finish (below) in the 1954 Mille Miglia on 2 May.

Ascari's appearances for Lancia in 1954 include competing in the Tourist Trophy on 11 September (left top and bottom). With co-driver Villoresi he retires. In April he and Lancia assist at the Swiss racing driver's school at Campione (right top and bottom). At Campione Alberto has the unusual opportunity to try out a 500cc Formula 3 Cooper (opposite).

In 1954, from top left clockwise, Alberto Ascari pays attention to American driver John Fitch before the Mille Miglia, attends the Swiss Grand Prix as a spectator in his Tyrolean hat, confers with team-mate Villoresi at Barcelona, and at Reims joins Onofre Marimon and a vivacious admirer.

Gianni Lancia arranges for his two aces to drive Maseratis in the French Grand Prix at Reims in July 1954. Ascari tries the car in practice (above) and in the race makes a rare indifferent start (below) to be alongside the Mercedes-Benz of Hans Herrmann.

A hint of what might have been in 1954 is provided by Alberto Ascari's one-off drive with Ferrari in the Italian Grand Prix on 5 September. In his Ferrari 625 Ascari leads every lap, with only two exceptions, from number seven to 48, when he draws into the pits, goggles raised, his engine expired. Neither Lampredi nor Meazza can restore him to the fray.

CHAPTER 8

Sunset in the park

For Alberto Ascari the year in which he turned 36 was a lost season, sent to try the patience of a dedicated sportsman. Italy's double World Champion was destined to race only seven times in 1954 and only four of those races were world-ranked Grands Prix. This tested his relationship with Mietta, who hoped to see him pack away his carefully-boxed racing kit one final time.

'Sometimes I would go and watch him race,' Mietta said. 'I used to hide in a corner of the pits hoping that the race would end quickly and Alberto would arrive safe and sound. But other times I would stay in Milan. When I waited at home that telephone became a terrible thing. To ease the tension I would play cards with my friends or go to the cinema with a female friend, because during those two hours I was not thinking about him racing, risking his life. I didn't want the children around me during these hours because I was very agitated. I wanted to be free to be nervous, sad or whatever without having to hide it from them.

A restorative swig of San Pellegrino is just the tonic for Ascari after his victory in the Grand Prix of Naples of 1955. None could have foreseen that this would be the final victory for a great Italian hero.

'When he returned,' Mietta continued, 'I knew what had happened by his mood. If everything had gone well you could see it on his face. Otherwise he was nervous because something had forced him to retire – or he had had a disagreement with another driver. Sometimes there was no need for words. Sometimes I asked him. But usually, on entering our flat, it had become of secondary importance. There were family problems and races were another issue.'

'There were two Alberto Ascaris,' said his friend Mila Schön, 'the sportsman and the family man. Two different and separate worlds, two different ways of life for him. He didn't talk about racing when at home, nor did he talk about his family at the tracks.' At times, said Schön, he didn't talk at all: 'Alberto was often taciturn. He could enjoy natural beauty without talking about it. He liked walking very much. I remember some nice strolls, from Santa Margherita to Paraggi, along the coast of the charming Tigullio Gulf, or round about Cortina, along forest paths. One or two hours of walking with not a word spoken. He just enjoyed the silence, the peace so far from the world of racing, or simply from the world with all its problems and tensions.'

Ascari's relationship with Schön became an important

part of his life. Born Mila Nutrizio, she was the sister of Nino Nutrizio, the journalist and editor whose comments about Alberto were quoted earlier. For a time she was married to amateur racing driver Aurelio Schön. His thus became the surname (meaning 'beautiful' in German) that the attractive Mila associated with her successful fashion designs and toiletries.

'I met Alberto in 1950 or 1951,' said Mila Schön. 'Gigi Villoresi introduced me to him. Alberto wasn't World Champion yet, but he was a very popular driver, so at first I was a bit timorous. But I soon realised how good-natured he was. Something happened between us that is very difficult and rare to see between a man and a woman: we were real friends, close friends. We began to see each other quite frequently at Milan or Cortina or Santa Margherita Ligure where we all had holiday houses.

'I was also friendly with Mietta,' added Mila. 'Mietta was well aware that I sometimes used to accompany Alberto to the races. I was a fan, a real racing buff. I saw him at Le Mans and at Reims, Monte Carlo and Berne, and of course at the most important Italian races, Monza and the Targa Florio. But she wasn't jealous at all. She knew that Alberto was deeply in love with her and that my friendship with him was something lived *en camarade* by the two of us.'

Alberto Ascari needed the love and loyalty of his male and female friends alike in the trying year 1954, which saw arch-rival Juan Fangio gallop away with the World Championship. 'Alberto Ascari became a champion by incessantly improving his natural talent, which was outstanding,' said mechanic Ener Vecchi. 'He wasn't easily satisfied. If he was dominating a race with a comfortable lead, he didn't lift his foot. He didn't spare the car – as Fangio used to do, for instance. He pressed on regardless.

'When testing,' Vecchi added, 'he was continuously and resolutely looking for the best way to go. He went on and on until the problem was solved.' Testing occupied much of Alberto's '54 season. His first drive of the new D50 on 20 February at Caselle Airport turned out to be far in advance of its race-readiness. Testing soon moved to San Remo, where the early spring of the Italian Riviera allowed comparative trials on a circuit that Lancia knew well. In May, when the mists and rain

cleared from Monza, the Lancia crew decamped to that famous and definitive track.

Neither roadholding nor braking were up to scratch for the major mid-summer races Alberto had hoped to enter. Braking was a particular bugbear with the special quadruple-shoe drum brakes that Vittorio Jano favoured. A braking fault contributed to a heavy crash of a test car at Monza, fortunately without serious injury to driver Ascari.

One of the key suppliers whom Ascari visited during that long summer of '54 was Milan's Pirelli. 'An Ascari in civilian clothes used to visit the offices in Viale Abruzzi,' a company author wrote, 'having come – as he used to say jokingly – on a duty call after a victory or with propitiatory intentions before facing a following race. This man, who had disciplined his youthful passion for engines, brought up amongst the garages and workshops of Milan, carried the burden of his fame extremely naturally. But we also remember his restlessness and discomfiture when he was forced to remain idle awaiting the Lancia.'

Not until early October 1954, after tests again at Caselle and San Remo, did the D50 seem ready to deliver competitive performance. Then it returned to Monza, wrote Rodney Walkerley: 'Reported that Ascari has taken the Grand Prix Lancia (2.5-litre V8) round Monza in 1min 56secs, which is not only 121.4mph but is faster than Fangio's Mercedes time in September of 1min 58.4secs.' This was more like it.

Buoyed by this performance, Lancia booked starting places for two cars in the Spanish GP at Barcelona on 26 October. It invited its drivers to meet the press in Turin on 14 October. On his way there from Milan, said Ascari, along the Autostrada 'I was overtaking a huge petrol tanker with what appeared to be a clear road in front when a lorry swung out, completely blocking my path. I couldn't swerve off the road because I was hemmed between two walls. I jammed on my brakes. The lorry rushed toward me like an express train. I just had time to feel my stomach turn over as when you fall from a roof in a dream … then I saw stars.'

Alberto still had a bandaged chin from this incident when, at Turin's Caselle, he briefly shook down one of the cars for Barcelona four days before the race. His son Tonino may never have seen his father race, but he came along that morning to watch Alberto turn a few laps in the Lancia. Alberto doffed his suit jacket and tried the unpainted racer in shirt and tie.

That the D50 was quick enough was demonstrated gloriously at Barcelona. Walkerley: 'The Lancias were rockets on wheels while they were going, as witness Ascari's practice lap, less than 2secs slower than Fangio's Alfa Romeo record (103.7mph) in 1951. Although Ascari was driving extremely hard, roadholding is good except under full throttle out of a curve.' Alberto put the cherry-red Lancia on pole with a lap a full second quicker than Fangio could manage with his Mercedes-Benz and Villoresi, fifth fastest, was a tick of the watch faster than Moss in a works-backed Maserati. Ascari was back where he belonged.

'The debut was sensational,' wrote Walkerley, 'into the lead after three laps and then into the paddock after nine, with the fastest lap of the day in the bag. The second car (Villoresi) started with no brakes and completed one lap only.' In fact Ascari was credited with ten laps after a final tour just to check that the Lancia really could not continue after the failure of a banal but essential part of the clutch mechanism. His fastest lap at Barcelona meant that his name appeared on the list of qualifiers for the 1954 World Championship – with that single solitary point. (To this he could add 0.14 of a point for sharing the fastest lap at Silverstone with six other drivers.)

A snowy 5 January 1955 found the whole Lancia team and five D50s back at Turin's Caselle Airport. They were there to load both cars and personnel aboard a four-engined Douglas DC6 leased from KLM. By flying the cars to Buenos Aires for the winter *Temporada*, said Gianni Lancia, his technicians gained time to ensure that they were properly prepared. He provided two spare cars and three racing cars for Ascari, Villoresi and Eugenio Castellotti, all of whom were entered in the Argentine GP in mid-January. At 10:26am, shrugging off slanting sleet, the DC6 took to the air.

No greater contrast with cold Caselle could have been imagined than the searing temperatures in which the season's first World Championship race was run at Buenos Aires. On tarmac rendered viscid by the heat, all three Lancias ultimately lost their grip and spun off to various degrees of damage. Alberto did so on the 21st of

96 laps, having led for many of the opening laps from the front row of the grid. Clearly a handful, his D50 went straight off and stubbed its nose against a fence.

Braking was still at the heart of the problem. Jano's pet brakes were powerful, but after a few laps they lost their balance and grabbed erratically, aggravating any handling instability. Both Ascari and Villoresi – used to the much more stable Ferrari brakes – urged changes, but the engineer was reluctant. He sought improvements while the Lancias were rebuilt for the European season which, now lacking a Formula 2, offered a number of non-championship Formula 1 races.

Lancia entered for three lesser contests before the first European points race at Monaco: Turin, Pau and Naples in March, April and May respectively. Turin, run over the Valentino Park circuit in Lancia's home town, was virtually a command performance. Lancia treated it as such and brought its full team. Ascari was on pole after qualifying but Jean Behra's Maserati was close, and the Maseratis were troublesome in the race until Alberto broke free of a pack of them and took a commanding lead which he held to the finish. It was his first win in a single-seater race since the Swiss GP in August 1953. Reliability was promising with his team-mates placing third and fourth.

Alberto's dance card was filling in nicely for 1955. Although Lancia was planning to compete in only a few sports-car races, it was releasing its drivers to handle sports cars of other makes. While Villoresi was planning to pilot Maseratis, Ascari was rejoining the Ferrari team with the handsome young man from Lodi, Eugenio Castellotti, as his co-driver. Excitement was considerable when they were announced as co-drivers of a new 4.4-litre six-cylinder Ferrari being built for Le Mans. An important preliminary race would be the 1,000 Kilometres of Monza on the weekend after Monaco.

'Ascari and his Lancia had the competition in his pocket from the start until just before the end' of the F1 race at Pau on Easter Monday in April, wrote Rodney Walkerley. 'Behra clung to his tail in the opening stages, but Ascari, competent motorist, began to draw away by one second per lap until he had nearly a minute in hand – and then a rear brake pipe split. After a long pit stop which cost him the race, he went on with front brakes only, and, we observed, without demanding Castellotti's car as a replacement.' Alberto was awarded fifth place and left Pau with both pole position and the fastest lap.

For Pau Lancia had installed more conventional two-shoe brakes. These were a help too at the Naples GP on 8 May. Its organisers attracted a small field with, however, works teams from Lancia and Maserati. From pole position with a time more than a second quicker than any rival Alberto Ascari leaped into the lead and kept it for the full 153 miles. Finishing second was Luigi Musso in a Maserati. Musso, with Castellotti and Cesare Perdisa, belonged to a new young generation of Italian lions who were clawing their way toward the higher levels of the sport.

Lancia now busied itself with the preparation of four cars for the first European championship GP on the Monte Carlo circuit on 22 May, two weeks after the Naples race. In the weekend between Naples and Monaco a light-hearted motorsports event was held in northern Italy – the second Cinema Rally. Most mobbed by the admiring public was Gina Lollobrigida with her husband. La Lollo's Alfa Romeo 1900 had to be diverted from the official route to prevent the total breakdown of civic order. Greeting the glamorous rallyists at their Como stopover was a relaxed Alberto Ascari, natty as usual in striped tie and double-breasted suit.

Alberto was back in his usual racing kit for the Monaco race the following weekend. Using new short-wheelbase cars built especially for this race Fangio and Moss put their Mercedes-Benzes on the front row, but splitting them was Ascari, who equalled Fangio for fastest lap in timed practice. Castellotti was in the second row and Villoresi in the third after being spun by a grabbing front brake.

At the cinema that evening 20th Century-Fox held the gala premiere of its new production, *The Racers*, the very film for which Ascari and Villoresi had motored around the Monegasque streets the summer before under the guidance of a second-unit director. They were subjected to much good-natured kidding by the other drivers and teams invited to the premiere.

The May evening was balmy as the drivers walked back to their hotels from the cinema. Strolling along the seafront, they passed the chicane set up by the organisers to make the cars zig-zag after emerging from the tunnel. One of the drivers pointed to the makeshift array of logs

and sandbags and said, 'Whoever touches that tomorrow will end up in the water.' Alberto Ascari could not resist. He was, said Fangio, 'both superstitious and sceptical'. True to both sides of his character, he walked over and touched a bit of iron on the barrier, the Italian equivalent of knocking on wood.

The Sunday of the Grand Prix brought glorious sunshine. Juan Fangio roared into the race lead and held it while the Milanese driver was running third or fourth. Before mid-race Fangio retired, however, leaving the lead to team-mate Moss. The Briton was threatening to lap Ascari, running second, when on lap 81 of 100 his Mercedes too retired. Just as Moss was drawing up to his pit in a cloud of smoke Ascari, out on the circuit, was approaching the chicane. He slowed as usual, only to have the left front brake seize, throwing the car askew. Oil from the Moss Mercedes gave Alberto no chance to regain control. His Lancia speared through barriers off the edge of the quay – missing two massive iron bollards – and plunged into the harbour not far from a moored yacht.

After many lengthy seconds the familiar blue helmet popped to the surface, Ascari under it. Stroking strongly for the shore and safety, he was collected by a launch. Taken to Monte Carlo Hospital, Alberto was found to be shaken, to be heavily bruised, especially on his right thigh, and to have light injuries on his nose and forehead. All in all he was a very lucky racing driver – not lucky enough, however, to have completed that lap and be told that he was the race's clear and easy leader.

Among his many visitors at the hospital was Mila Schön: 'I went to the Ferrari pit after the race, asking about his condition. Castellotti told me Alberto wasn't so bad and gave me a lift to the hospital. He was sitting in his bed. He had a tray on his knees and was eating a grapefruit. I cheered him, joking: "You were so eager to take a bath?" He laughed, shaking his head. I soon took my leave because I had to go to Paris. "Don't worry," he said. "I'll see you in a few days back in Milan."'

On the Tuesday after the race he was released from hospital. 'Gianni Lancia sent a chauffeur-driven car to take us back to Milan,' Mietta Ascari recalled. 'En route we went to see a site on the Riviera where a friend of ours planned to build holiday villas, and then back home. On our arrival at Corso Sempione we were very amused to find that the Italian Motor Nautical Federation had presented him with a life jacket for future races – just in case!' He also opened an envelope to find a certificate that proclaimed him an honorary member of a society of frogmen.

Wednesday saw Alberto Ascari at the Lancia branch in Milan, where they made some repairs to his road car. His leg was bothering him, so he asked his friend Gilberto Colombo to do the driving. At ten o'clock on the Thursday morning the phone rang at Corso Sempione 60. Eugenio Castellotti was calling from Monza, where he had been testing a Ferrari 750S for the race that weekend. 'Alberto was sleeping,' Mietta remembered. 'Speaking from his bed, I heard him say, "Yes, all right, I'll come up. I'll probably arrive before midday." Alberto then told me that Castellotti had invited him to watch some trials up at Monza. He got up calmly, had breakfast, did his toilet and just before he left told me, "I'll be back home by one o'clock, so you can make some lunch".'

The driver donned his usual shirt, tie and jacket and made for Monza, arriving about half an hour before noon. Castellotti had completed some tests of the unpainted 750S 'Monza' Ferrari, which was not yet rivalling the speed of the Maserati that Villoresi was driving. Alberto chatted with Giovanni Lurani, who remembered the day: 'It was a beautiful May afternoon and the Monza track in its spring colours seemed even more beautiful than usual. There was an air of absolute calm, a peaceful silence on that vast site.'

Sitting in the Grandstand Restaurant with friends, Ascari nibbled a bread roll and drank some tea during the mid-day break. To his friends, Lurani said, he spoke 'with his acute and calm knowledge and confident experience about the technical and sporting consequences of the recent Grand Prix and the effects they would have on future races. Alberto assessed men and events, made plans, gave advice and joked with that good-natured wit that made him dear to all those who knew him.'

One of his concerns at Monza, his friends well knew, was the fast left-hand Vialone bend at the back of the circuit. Speaking to the managers there he had once said, in his joking way, 'I would feel much happier if you could widen it with a little asphalt!' Paving was missing, he felt, at a point on the periphery. 'He had requested

and obtained from the organisers a very special thing: some 80 centimetres of asphalt added to the unpaved verge in order to go through flat out,' said driver Gino Munaron.

The break over, Alberto and Eugenio went to inspect the Ferrari. Glancing at Lurani, Ascari said rhetorically, 'It's best to get straight back into a car after an accident, isn't it?' Taking off his jacket, he settled stiffly into its seat. Checking the controls as was his habit, he looked at the Ferrari mechanics and said, 'I'd like to try her out – just to see if I'm okay for Sunday. I'll only make three or four laps. I'll drive slowly!' Hearing no objection, he borrowed Castellotti's helmet, goggles and gloves and tucked his tie into his shirt front. With two girls, Eugenio and the Ferrari he posed for a photographer at 12:25 before starting the engine and driving out on the familiar lane from the paddock to the track.

No friend of Ascari's could understand what compelled him to drive this strange car so soon after his accident and especially without the racing kit that was part and parcel of his persona. His wife thought she knew the reason: 'He was overcome by curiosity. Being curious and wanting to test things was part of his character. He'd been away from Ferrari for a year and a half. The temptation to learn of any advances made and possibly compare them with the Lancia was too strong.' Ascari had never driven a car of this type. He had not driven a sports-racing car of any kind since the previous September. Nor had he driven a racing car on the Belgian Englebert tyres with which the Monza was fitted.

The Ferrari, he found, was no pussycat. In agility it was the complete antithesis of the lithe Lancia he'd been racing. 'That car was really dangerous,' said Gino Munaron of the Monza. 'I can speak from experience.' Another who could do the same was driver/journalist Paul Frère. 'As so many drivers have discovered to their cost,' wrote Frère, 'the Monza Ferrari does not forgive a mistake and leaves no loophole.' Before a crash in Sweden, he related, 'I knew that an accident was inevitable as the car had taken complete charge of the situation.'

Castellotti had lapped Monza at 113mph. Alberto averaged 96 for his first lap and 109mph for his second. By his standards he was 'driving slowly'. Congenitally incapable of driving slowly, however, on his third lap he pressed harder. He was quicker through the right-hand Lesmo turns, then faster approaching the Vialone left bend, where more asphalt had been provided so he could take it flat out. But the Ferrari wanted to use all that added pavement – and more. Ascari, surprised by its stubbornness, drawing deeply on reactions he had not expected to need that sunny midday, tried to rein it in, only to have the car snap sideways, its tyres howling, then overturn and bounce, chaotically, flinging its driver out before it clattered to rest against a fence far down the left side of the track. It was not yet one o'clock.

'The roar of the car turned into a series of crashes followed by the terrible silence that seals tragedies,' said Giovanni Lurani. The incredible, impossible, unthinkable had happened. Like his father, Alberto Ascari had been 'tempted ... charmed by speed.' Like his father, he had been unable to resist that ultimate temptation.

Rushing to the scene, his friends found Alberto grievously wounded in the grass. His faint pulse detected, he was stretchered aboard an ambulance in which, Gigi Villoresi at his side, he expired. 'He died of multiple injuries,' wrote Kevin Desmond, 'including a smashed skull, a fractured jaw, completely fractured left shoulder, completely fractured pelvis and so on. He had virtually been crushed to death.' His death was declared to have been at 1:05pm – about when the bourgeois Ascari, accustomed to his comforts, was expected home for lunch.

'That midday, eating and chatting with the children, I felt no terrible premonitions,' said Mietta Ascari. 'It was neither a race day nor a day of practice. He had only gone up there to watch the trials – not to drive. Therefore I was calm. Then this friend arrived, the husband of Mila Schön, and told me that Alberto had been involved in a bad accident at Monza, and that I had best go up there with him.' Their visit was to the simple chapel at the Monza Hospital where the corpse of Alberto Ascari had been laid out.

All Italy mourned. The great and good came to Monza to pay their respects. The solemn transfer of his coffin from Monza to Milan drew silent kilometres of people whose lives he had touched. His funeral took place at the church of San Carlo al Corso on the morning of Saturday, 28 May. Among the pallbearers were Eugenio Castellotti, Paolo Marzotto, Umberto Maglioli and members of the Scuderia Ambrosiana. Gigi Villoresi and Mietta Ascari grieved together. The long, slow funeral cortege passed Corso Sempione 60, where Ascari's mother Elisa gestured a goodbye from the balcony. Alberto's remains were placed next to those of his father in the family tomb.

Milan's automobile club set up a fund to honour the memory of Ascari. When closed at mid-year it had received almost 23 million lire, equal to some $34,000. Lancia contributed five million, Fiat two million and Ferrari and Maserati one million lire each.

Thinking at first that it would somehow manage to continue in racing after this devastating loss, Lancia negotiated the services of Mike Hawthorn as its new team leader. Soon, however, Lancia announced that it was suspending all sporting activity. After negotiations all six of its beautiful D50s, the cars that Ascari helped develop, and all their supporting equipment were handed over to Ferrari. Mike Hawthorn would race one after all. Eugenio Castellotti also joined the Ferrari strength. Gigi Villoresi returned to Maserati and retired from racing in 1956.

'So far everything seems to be only an ugly dream,' Mietta Ascari wrote to Enzo Ferrari that July of 1955, 'and I still have the impression that he will be back from one of his usual trips to America and that everything will again be as it was before. But when I think that I can never again look forward to his return, I feel I shall go mad and, were there not the children who need me, I should certainly have gone to join my Alberto.' She too is now gone. Thanks to her and Ascari's many friends, however, wonderful memories remain of the racer who was charmed by speed.

Rudy Mailander captures Alberto Ascari cornering hard at the Station Hairpin in the Grand Prix of Europe at Monte Carlo on 22 May 1955. Never again will he drive the magnificent Lancia D50.

Gianni Lancia counts on Alberto Ascari to press his new D50 Grand Prix car to the limit to expose its weaknesses, as he does in a series of tests at San Remo's Ospedaletti circuit in *December 1954. Ascari hearkens to the views of engineer Vittorio Jano while development driver Navone leans on the Lancia's distinctive side-mounted fuel tank.*

Giuseppe Navone leans over the cockpit while the fuel is checked on the final 1954 version of the Lancia D50 as it is given a test (opposite) by Ascari at Turin's Caselle Airport.

In this form Ascari races the D50 for the first time at Barcelona in the Spanish Grand Prix on 14 October. In the race he is leading the Ferrari of eventual winner Mike Hawthorn.

The first 1955 challenge for the Lancia team is the Argentine Grand Prix on 16 January. Anything but manageable in the *Buenos Aires heat, Alberto Ascari's D50 retires after a crash at just over one-fifth distance.*

The citizens of Turin turn out in strength to see Ascari start in their GP on 27 March alongside the Maseratis of Jean Behra (8) *and Luigi Musso* (34). *After a stirring battle with the Maserati of Roberto Mieres he prevails to take the victory.*

At Pau on 11 April 1955 Ascari leads easily (above) until delayed by brake-pipe repairs. Before the race at Monte Carlo in May (opposite) Jano and Ascari are joined by Mercedes- *Benz team manager Alfred Neubauer, right, who enlivens the proceedings by pulling out his wallet to make a cash bid on the spot for the driver's services.*

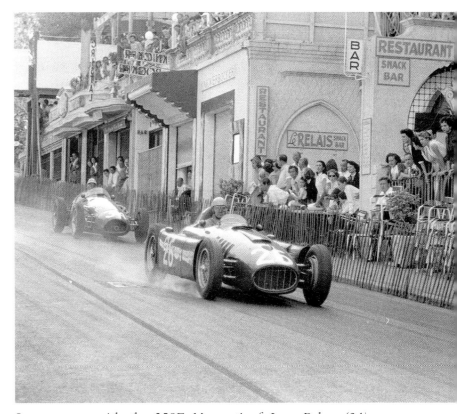

Rudy Mailander portrays scenes from the final motor race of Alberto Ascari at Monaco on 22 May 1955. He is entering and leaving the fast left-hand bend outside the Hotel de Paris (opposite), with its road sign prohibiting speed and noise.

In company with the 250F Maserati of Jean Behra (34), Ascari locks a front wheel on the descent to Mirabeau – a foretaste of the erratic braking that sends him plunging into the harbour waters.

Many experts then and later seek to make sense of the skid marks on the exit from Monza's Vialone bend that end abruptly when the 750S Monza Ferrari driven by Alberto Ascari commences the tumbling and rolling that leave it a crumpled wreck on the left side of the track.

Found upside-down, it is put back on its wheels by appalled onlookers. Like all other fans of the great Ascari, they prefer to remember him as he is pictured by Günther Molter during practice for his last race at Monte Carlo (overleaf). Both the man and his talent are greatly missed.

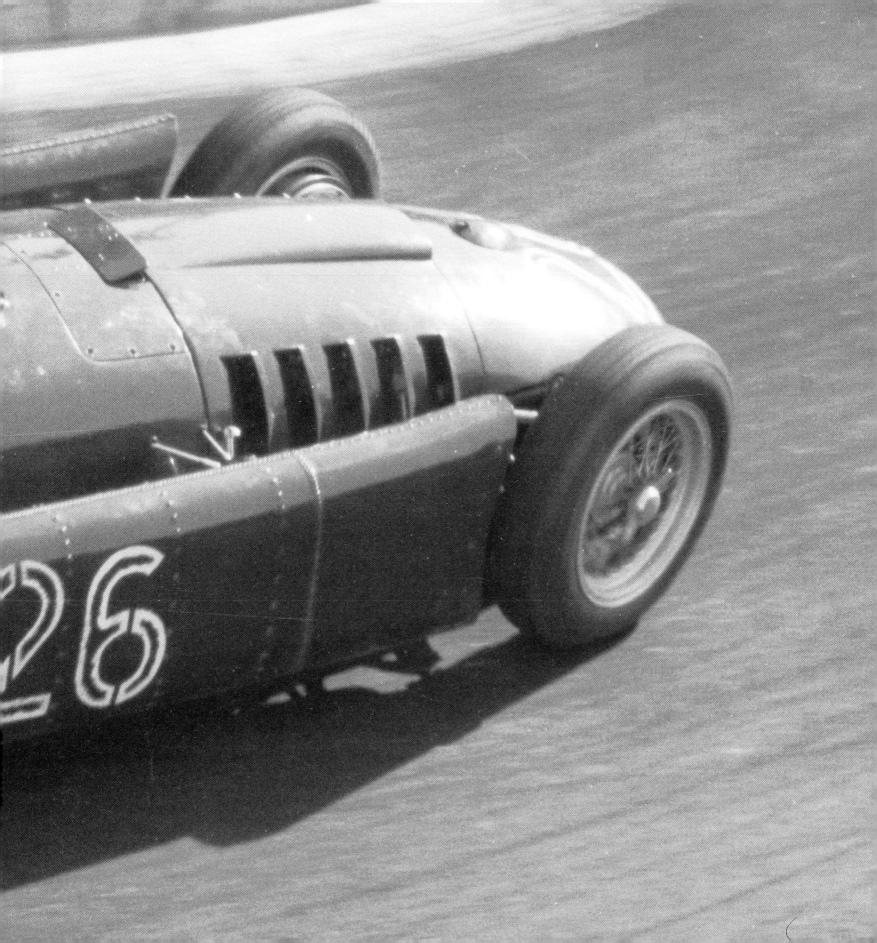

Annotated bibliography

Ascari, Alberto 'Mi Batterò per il Titolo' (*Tempo*, Issue 6, 1954). 1p, 1 photograph

After the furore over his leaving Ferrari for Lancia at the end of 1953 Ascari gives his reasons in his own words to the readers of *Tempo*.

Bertarelli, Franco 'Faccio tre giri e torno subito' (*Incom*, 1955). 4pp, 9 photographs

Insightful and personal portrait of the driver and his career written after his death, emphasising the calm of his home life.

Canestrini, Giovanni 'L'Anno di Alberto Ascari' (*L'Automobile*, January 1958). 1p, 4 photographs

Celebrates the 1951 season in which Ascari comes dramatically to the fore, and tells the story of his strategy for a 'surprise' pit stop in that year's German GP.

Cimarosti, Adriano *Carrera Panamericana 'Mexico'* (Automobilia, Milan, 1987). 381pp, many photographs and drawings

Excellent history in Italian, English, and French of this great contest that provides fine detail on the background of Ascari's participation there in 1951, when he is second with Villoresi, and 1952, when he crashes out early.

Clymer, Floyd et al *1952 Indianapolis 500 Mile Race Yearbook* (Floyd Clymer, Los Angeles, 1952). 112 pp, many photographs and charts.

Indispensable softback reference to each year's Indy race, compiled in the years when author and publisher Clymer was still originating special material on the events of qualifying and the race. Contains the authoritative reporting of Russ Catlin on the profound positive impact that the skill and personality of Ascari made on the not-easily-impressed Americans.

Cossa, Valeria 'Che vita veloce con "Ciccio" Ascari' (*Ruoteclassiche*, July/August 1990). 2pp, 7 photographs

Valuable interview conducted with Mietta Ascari, speaking about relationships with Ferrari and Lancia. Illustrations include a photo of her and Enzo Ferrari autographed by the latter that did not prevent her from remembering him as a 'hard' man.

Davis, Melton S. 'Preparava la corsa come un battaglia' (*Settimo Giorno*, 1955). 4pp, 4 photographs

After Ascari's death the Italian weekly published this translation of an extract from an article by Davis that appeared in *Adam* of February 1954 and called it the article that Ascari considered the 'most precise' of all that had been written about him. In the extract Ascari speaks of his driving techniques in some detail. Now living in Rome, Davis well remembered the racer, whom he considered 'quite a guy'.

De Agostini, Cesare *Antonio e Alberto Ascari* (L'Editrice dell'Automobile, Milan, 1968). 95pp

An important history that combines the stories of the father and son and concludes with the coincidences between their lives and deaths. More a history of their racing than an in-depth portrait, it is an important source for the later work of Kevin Desmond (*qv*). Provides a unique detailed listing of the races of Alberto Ascari on both two wheels and four, missing only the 12 Hours of Casablanca in 1953.

Desmond, Kevin *The Man with Two Shadows – The Story of Alberto Ascari* (Proteus, London and New York, 1981). 178pp, 12 photographs

The wonderful title of Desmond's pioneering book about Ascari in English refers to the shadow of his father as well as his own that Alberto was required to cast through the early years of his career. Has the indispensable value of Kevin's interviews with such leading players in the drama as Mietta Ascari, Gigi Villoresi, and Aurelio Lampredi.

Ferrari, Enzo *My Terrible Joys* (Hamish Hamilton, London, 1963). 164pp, 47 photographs

Early British-style publication – translated by Ivan Scott – of the personal story of Enzo, who always confessed to being a frustrated journalist. Not surprisingly he is acute in his observations about Ascari, whom he considered 'unusual, both as man and driver'.

Fitch, John with Nolan, William F. *Adventure on Wheels* (G.P. Putnam's Sons, New York, 1959). 284pp, 38 photographs

As this book demonstrates, Fitch is one of the few racing drivers who can write really well. He relates the story of Ascari and Villoresi arriving in Monte Carlo to drive cars in scenes for the film *The Racers*.

Frère, Paul *On the Starting Grid* (B.T. Batsford, London, 1957). 224pp, 57 photographs plus a drawing of the Spa circuit on which the author scored many successes

The author's story of his racing career from his first motor-cycle contest in 1939 through 1956, when he was second in a Ferrari in the Belgian GP. Frère always balanced his racing with his journalistic commitments and made the most of some excellent drives. His vivid description of a crash in a Ferrari Monza at Sweden's Kristianstad circuit in 1955 helped convince the author of this book that the car deserves most of the blame for Ascari's fatal crash that same year in another Monza.

Gregori, Giorgio *Segreti di Corridori* (L'Editrice dell'Automobile, Milan, 1968). 191pp, 33 photographs

In a book touching on the careers of a number of drivers, Gregori provides a brief but attractive history of Ascari's life and drives on pages 55 to 73.

Hamilton, Duncan with Scott, Lionel *Touch Wood!* (Speed and Sports Publications, London, 1971). 229pp, 57 photographs

Originally written in 1960, this is an engaging narrative of Hamilton's racing career, albeit sanitised in the style of the day. He vividly describes the 1953 Le Mans race in which he and Rolt had an epic battle with the Ferrari of Ascari and Villoresi.

Hawthorn, Mike *Challenge Me the Race* (William Kimber, London, 1958). 240pp, 31 photographs

Thanks to Chris Nixon's research and writing we now know much more about the career of Hawthorn, but this book remains an important source of his thoughts. Unlike Moss he considered Ascari to be faster than Fangio and had authoritative views on the reason for the fatal crash at Monza.

Heglar, Mary Schnall *The Grand Prix Champions* (Bond Parkhurst Books, 1973). 234pp, 102 photographs

A pot pourri of World Champions from 1950 to 1972 which gives 12 pages to Ascari's life, concentrating on superstitions and coincidences.

Klemantaski, Louis *Klemantaski Himself* (Palawan Press, London, 1998). 396pp, many photographs

Fascinating because it is highly personal and beautifully illustrated by this fine photographer, it contains the charming story – told to the author's disadvantage – of Ascari pointing out the Ferrari Barchetta's novel fifth forward speed.

Lurani, Giovanni 'Alberto Ascari' (*Auto Italiana*, 30 May 1955). 2 pp

Touching tribute to a fallen friend, whom Lurani had met at the funeral of Antonio Ascari in 1925.

Millanta, Corrado 'Alberto Ascari' (*Quattroruote*, June 1975). 5 pp, 6 photographs

Commemoration of the career and life of Ascari, published on the 20th anniversary of his death. Provides pungent personal recollections of the driver by one of Italy's leading photojournalists who was dragooned by Ascari into accompanying him on his 'training runs' over the dark and foggy Lombardy countryside.

Molter, Günther (translated by Charles Meisl) *Juan Manuel Fangio, World Champion* (G.T. Foulis, 1956). 184pp, 62 photographs

This is a good book which rather oddly stops after the 1955 British Grand Prix. Molter visits Ascari in Milan and depicts the atmosphere of his flat at Corso Sempione 60.

Moss, Stirling, face to face with Purdy, Ken *All But My Life* (William Kimber, 1963). 239pp, 18 photographs

Post-Goodwood-accident look at the Moss legend in conversation with American Ken Purdy. Gives the views of spectator Moss on the relative styles of Fangio and Ascari.

Nutrizio, Nino 'Scappò da due collegi per correre in motoci-cletta' (*Incom*, February 1951). 1p, 1 photograph

A capsule summary of Ascari's career with some attractive anecdotes, written on the threshold of his breakthrough season by the brother of Mila Schön, who became an important lady friend of Alberto.

Rancati, Gino *Ferrari – a Memory* (Motorbooks International, Osceola, 1959). 198pp, 20 photographs

Memoir of Enzo Ferrari by a journalist friend (if Ferrari could be said to have friends) who quotes Villoresi on the break-up of the relationship of the two drivers with Ferrari at the end of the 1953 season.

Rimini, Ing. Giorgio 'Ricordando Antonio Ascari' (*L'Auto Italiana*, 31 August, 30 September, and 15 October 1955). 17pp, 24 photographs

Intimate and detailed portrait of Alberto Ascari's father, written by an engineer with the Alfa Romeo company who was close to the elder Ascari's racing exploits. Gives valuable insights into his character and his life and death.

Roebuck, Nigel *Grand Prix Greats* (Patrick Stephens Limited, 1986). 216pp, 149 photographs and 25 colour portrait paintings by Craig Warwick

The author chose 25 drivers for his book which included Ascari, whose death was reported in his local evening paper as 'Milan: Ascari, racing driver, killed in crash.' Wrote Roebuck, 'It seemed scarcely credible they could be talking about the Ascari. A handful of words to dismiss a man of such gift?' Roebuck makes up for this slight with a concise portrait of Ascari.

Schuler, Steve *Alberto Ascari Racing Career* (Auto Racing Analysis, racelaunch@aol.com).

A fully tabulated and annotated list of Ascari's car racing career compiled specifically for this book project, giving venue, date, car driven, qualifying position, results and/or reasons for retirement.

Serra, Franco 'Guidò per la prima volta seduto sulle ginocchia del padre' (*Incom*, 1955, Issues 11 and 12). 7pp, 13 photographs

A personal portrait of the driver after his untimely death, with a good overview of his family life and his battles with Fangio.

Sheldon, Paul and Rabagliati, Duncan *A Record of Grand Prix and Voiturette Racing – Volumes 4, 5 and 6* (St Leonard's Press, Shipley, 1987, 1988, 1993)

Although not complete in all respects (race numbers are sometimes missing) these carefully-prepared volumes are essential for any historian writing about motor racing. There are no illustrations but the text is often vivid.

Taruffi, Piero *Works Driver* (Temple Press Books, London, 1964). 222pp, 20+ photographs

Like Ascari a racer on two wheels and four, Taruffi was also an exceptional technician of all aspects of racing and record-breaking who drove for Mercedes in 1955 and Chevrolet (yes!) in 1957. He was instrumental in providing Ascari's first single-seater drive.

Villoresi, Luigi 'Requiem per un Grande Amico' (*Settimo Giorno*, 1955). 4pp, 10 photographs

Understandably emotional and personal tribute to a lost comrade by the man who helped cultivate Ascari's racing career, written immediately after his death. At the next event, he concluded, 'I will look out for him, as I always did at races, but to no avail. Poor Alberto!'

In addition to these specific citations the pages of many contemporary periodicals have contributed to this telling of the Ascari story. Among them are *The Motor*, *The Autocar*, *Speed Age*, *Settimo Giorno*, *Il Giorno*, *Auto Italiana*, *Auto Moto Sport*, *Interauto*, *Motor Sport*, *Motorsport* and *Autosport*. These have been accessed in the Ludvigsen Library in London and in the Museo dell'Automobile Carlo Biscaretti di Ruffia in Turin. I am also indebted to G. Fred Leydorf for his personal communication of a sketch by Aurelio Lampredi showing exactly where the hub of Ascari's wheel broke at Indianapolis.

Photograph credits

Bernard Cahier: P138, P150 upper & middle, P158 lower left, P176 lower left, P178 upper left, P195 lower, P198 upper & lower.

Yves Debraine: P106.

Kevin Desmond Collection: P18 lower, P19 lower left, P20 upper, P65 lower left, P86 lower left, P121, P122 upper.

Archivio Ferrari: Front endpaper, P21 lower, P47, P49 upper, P52 lower, P53 upper & lower, P55 upper left & right, lower left & right, P58 upper, P59 upper left & right, P64 lower left, P80–81 lower, P83 upper, P86 lower right, P87 lower right, P88–89, P94, P98 lower, P99, P113, P126 lower right, P127 upper left & right, P128, P135 left, P146 lower left & right, P148, P150 lower, P152–153, P178 lower left, P199.

Geoffrey Goddard: P34 lower, P51 lower, P78 upper, P84 lower, P129 lower, P157 upper left, P176 lower right.

Guy Griffiths: P97, P98 upper, P107 upper left & right.

The GP Library: P191 upper.

F.B. Kirbus from Cimarosti Collection: P109.

The Klemantaski Collection/T.C. March: P103.

Dave Knox from Tronolone Collection: P100–101 upper.

Ludvigsen Library: P8, P18 upper, P19 lower right, P34 upper, P35, P36 lower, P40, P48 upper & lower, P49 lower, P50, P51 upper, P52 upper, P56 right, P63 upper right, P84 upper, P85, P92 lower, P94 left, P127 lower, P134 lower, P147 upper, P151 upper, P154 left & right, P155, P157 upper right, P158 upper right, P172, P174 upper left & lower left, P190, P191 lower.

Maurice Louche: P38–39, P86 upper right, P129 upper, P134 upper, P136.

Rodolfo Mailander from Ludvigsen Library: Frontispiece, rear endpaper, P58 lower, P59 lower left & right, P60–61, P62, P63 upper left, lower left & right, P64 upper left & right & lower right, P65 upper left & right & lower right, P66 upper & lower, P67, P68, P75, P76 left & right, P77, P78 lower, P79, P80–81 upper, P82 upper left & lower left & right, P87 upper left & right & lower left, P90 upper left & right & lower left & right, P91, P92 upper left & right, P93 upper left & right & lower, P95 right, P122 lower, P123, P124–125, P130 lower right, P131 left & right, P132–133, P135 right, P137, P145 upper & lower, P146 upper left & right, P147 lower, P149, P151 lower, P156 left & right, P157 lower left & right, P158 upper left & lower right, P159, P160–161, P162, p169, P170 upper & lower left & right, P171 upper & lower, P173 upper & lower, P174 upper right & lower right, P175, P176 upper left & right, P177 upper left & right & lower, P178 upper right & lower right, P179, P187, P188 upper & lower, P189, P195 upper & middle, P196 upper & lower, P197 upper left & right & lower left & right.

Archivio Maserati: P29, P30 lower, P36 upper, P37 upper left & lower right, P130 lower left, P193 upper & lower.

Corrado Millanta: P30 upper, P32 lower, P33 upper & lower, P34 middle.

Günther Molter: P100–101 lower, P102, P104–105, P107 lower left & right, P108, P110, P111, P112, P126 upper left & right, P192 upper & lower, P200–201.

Museo dell'Automobile Carlo Biscaretti di Ruffia: P17, P20 lower, P21 upper, P37 lower left, P54, P56 left, P57 upper, P82 upper right, P83 lower, P96, P114, P180.

Spitzley/Zagari Collection: P10, P19 upper left & right, P22, P32 upper, P57 lower, P86 upper left, P126 lower left, P130 upper right.

Zagari/Testi: P31, P37 upper right, P130 upper left.

Index